B2B Customer Insight

The Proven Path to Growth

I0033721

B2B Customer Insight

The Proven Path to Growth

by

John Barrett
Priority Metrics Group, Inc.

≡IAP

Information Age Publishing, Inc.
Charlotte, North Carolina • www.infoagepub.com

Library of Congress Cataloging-in-Publication Data

Barrett, John, 1961-
  B2B customer insight : the proven path to growth / by John Barrett.
     p. cm.
  Includes bibliographical references.
  ISBN 978-1-61735-986-6 (paperback) — ISBN 978-1-61735-987-3 (hardcover) —
ISBN 978-1-61735-988-0 (e-book) 1. Customer relations. 2. Marketing. I.
Title.
  HF5415.5.B3687 2012
  658.8'04—dc23

                                                                    2012027937

Copyright © 2012 IAP–Information Age Publishing, Inc.

All rights reserved. No part of this publication may be reproduced, stored in a retrieval system, or transmitted in any form or by any electronic or mechanical means, or by photocopying, microfilming, recording or otherwise without written permission from the publisher.

Printed in the United States of America

CONTENTS

INTRODUCTION

Customer insight is a key part of our whole marketing program. If you want to stay in a leadership position, it is a great tool. It creates a partnership with the customer and makes them a part of the decision-making process.
—Jack McBride
CEO
Contec

The customer is always right.

That is the ultimate business cliché. It gets repeated so often that it almost loses its meaning.

The fact is, however, the customer *is* always right when it comes to finding the most effective ways to grow your business. This is especially true in the B2B world, where you are generally selling a much bigger share of your output to a much lower number of buyers than in the consumer world. That means that each company that purchases from you looms that much larger over your income statement—and you *must* find the methods to keep those customers as satisfied as possible, or risk layoffs, plant closings and even bankruptcy.

That risk is not necessary. When you know what your customers are thinking, when you understand what they value and how high they measure value, you can adjust your products and services accordingly to not only meet their needs, but anticipate them. And you might not even have to make any changes to what you sell—you might just have to change *how* you sell it. Many times, your customers are simply not aware of everything you provide as a supplier. When that is the case, it is just a matter of educating your customers to those hidden benefits.

B2B Customer Insight: The Proven Path to Growth, pp. vii–xi
Copyright © 2012 by Information Age Publishing
All rights of reproduction in any form reserved.

Gaining the complete customer understanding necessary to making the right strategic moves is the tricky part. Sometimes what your customers say is not what they really mean—and they may not even be aware of the discrepancy. Sometimes your customers are not completely honest with you—and one day, you wake up to find that your ongoing order just went to another supplier. Other times, the right questions simply are not asked of the customer—so you never get the real answers you require.

That is where customer insight comes into play. As president of Priority Metrics Group, Inc. (PMG for short), I have seen firsthand just how valuable this critical tool can be to our clients. For 2 decades, my team and I have provided customer insight surveys to suppliers in an incredible array of different industries. That vast experience has led us to many profound conclusions about how B2B businesses can optimize customer relationships, expand market share with those customers and even conquer completely new customer sectors by building on their existing capabilities to furnish new products.

I feel this information is too crucial not to share with the business world at large, which is why I have written this book. My mission here is to explain the importance of customer insight, and to reveal just how it provides real-world actionable strategies to both currently successful businesses that want to continue to grow, as well as companies facing hard times and hard choices. These continue to be volatile economic times and every business needs as much firepower as possible to meet the ongoing challenges constantly presenting themselves.

This book is especially necessary because, frankly, B2B customer research information is just not readily available through other avenues. There are an incredible number of consumer research firms out there, as well as many talented consumer research authorities retained in-house by companies—but that level of expertise does not have an equivalency in the B2B world. You will not find many third party firms that specialize in B2B customer insight and, even within the marketing department of large manufacturers, distributors, wholesalers or other B2B firms you will not find many executives familiar with even the survey basics.

That is a shame and a danger. As I mentioned earlier, B2B marketers face a customer base that is smaller and individual customers that carry much greater importance. To not thoroughly research what they value and how to best deliver those attributes can be akin to a supplier committing business suicide. The irony here is that it can be a lot easier, faster and cheaper to generate B2B customer insight than consumer insight. You are not dealing with millions of buyers spread out over the world—in some cases, you are only dealing with three or four!

And yet, customer insight surveys specially tailored to the B2B world are a rarity. Usually, consumer research methodologies are simply lazily adapted under the assumption that the rules are the same. They are not. And they differ in five important ways:

1) The size of the customer populations

As just noted, a supplier's customer population can easily be dominated by a handful of companies, as opposed to the overwhelming number of consumers out there. Obviously, that supplier needs to know not only what each one of those customers is after, but what their competition is up to as well. In the consumer world customer populations are measured in the millions. In the B2B world, customer populations are measured in the hundreds or even single digits. If one individual consumer switches brands, the marketer will not notice. If one B2B customer switches suppliers, it could mean layoffs and plant closures.

2) Product knowledge

Imagine a consumer buying a toothbrush. He or she almost never knows all that much about that toothbrush—how it got made, what technically went into the manufacturing process or what the quality level is. The consumer will just usually rely on a brand name they trust to infer a level of quality that causes them to feel more secure about the purchase. B2B is a very different story. Customers are incredibly knowledgeable about the products they order from suppliers; in many cases, they are subcontracting products they could actually make or have made themselves. They know what you are manufacturing inside out and have the experts in place who can thoroughly question every aspect of your process. In many cases they know the product cost as well as their supplier and will attempt to dictate—through contractual negotiations—what is an acceptable return on investment.

3) The magnitude of purchase volumes

When a consumer buys a toothbrush, he or she usually buys only one. When one of our clients, Bob Barker Company, sells toothbrushes to a customer, it is by the truckload. That is because their clients have thousands of people in huge detention facilities who require toothbrushes on a daily basis. While consumer companies focus on relatively small sales amid a sea of transactions, B2B companies routinely deal with one customer buying millions of dollars of product. Obviously, a survey methodology has to understand and anticipate that fact.

4) **The complexity of purchase transactions**

Let us go back to the example of the consumer buying a toothbrush. He or she will find the aisle where toothbrushes are sold, and then make a series of small decisions very quickly. Should it be a soft, medium or hard brush? The long reach-around stem or a traditional straight, short one? Blue, red, yellow or pink? None of these choices is a big deal; the toothbrush is just a couple of bucks and they will be getting a new one in a few weeks anyway. In the B2B world, that kind of fast and simple decision-making just does not happen, because there is a lot more transaction complexity in the supplier-customer relationship. That transaction complexity may involve multiple levels of employees interacting on both sides, as well as some very long-term internal discussions—and simple consumer surveys do not account for that at all.

5) **The buyer-seller relationship**

Do you think our consumer will ever meet someone from the company that made the toothbrush he or she just bought? Doubtful, unless they live in the same town. The consumer relationship to the seller is at arm's length and usually only addressed by research and surveys. In the B2B world, suppliers and customers, in contrast, usually have a very tight and entangled relationship. Their people actually talk and meet. And when a B2B survey is taken, it is highly visible— as a matter of fact, it almost turns into a two-way communication that is moderated by the survey company. The consumer and B2B methodologies, again, are completely different.

We have illustrated these five key differences in the below graphic, so you can get an overall sense of the wide gulf that exists between B2B and consumer transactions.

In the following chapters, we will look generally at why some suppliers grow and why others either shrink or just stand still. We will then detail the key questions that a customer insight survey should answer, what those findings mean and how to correctly interpret them. In addition, we will share what PMG's experience over the 20 years of doing these surveys has revealed about how suppliers should approach their customer relationships and what they can do to ensure the best possible customer insight on their own.

Finally, to fully illustrate how customer insight can make for an incredibly positive impact on a supplier's growth and sales, we will share real-life case studies featuring many of our valued clients. These are suppliers who realized the value of the data PMG provided—and successfully used it to both enhance their relationships with existing customers and build

PMG recognizes the important differences B2C and B2B markets in survey design:

Consumer Markets

- Many customers
- Limited product knowledge
- Small purchase quantities
- Relatively simple transactions
- Limited supplier relationships

Business Markets

- Fewer customers
- Substantial product knowledge
- Large purchase quantities
- Potentially complex transactions
- Close supplier relationships

Consumer Surveys

- Focus on the opposite picture
- Selective sample orientation

Business Surveys

- Focus on the individual customer
- Selective census opportunity

Figure 1.   Consumer and business-to-business markets.

relationships with new ones. I am grateful to them for allowing us to use their real names in this book, so that we are able to demonstrate how the practical application of customer insight is actually accomplished.

I have gotten quite an education in the past 20 years working with world class suppliers to provide them with the best possible customer insight, so that they might realize the best possible outcomes. I hope that you, the reader, will find the results of that education, found in this book, informative, enlightening and, most importantly, profitable.

CHAPTER 1

THE THREE THREATS TO GROWTH

When you are finished changing, you are finished.

—Benjamin Franklin

ANONYMOUS CASE STUDY: RESEARCH REQUIRES AN AUDIENCE

It was a big company with a solid history of success. It, at that time, employed more people than any other business in its region of the state. It is also a company whose name I will not share for reasons you will soon understand.

The CEO had requested that our company, Priority Metrics Group, Inc., do a customer insight survey—in my mind, *the* most important tool a company can use to determine its future direction and what current changes need to be initiated.

The results of the survey we did indicated that changes did indeed need to be made—and the sooner the better. What worked for this company in the past was definitely not going to continue to work much longer. I hoped that our presentation of the survey would hammer that point home, because decisive action had to be taken quickly.

So we all gathered in the company's boardroom, my team and the top management of the firm. And, as I made my way through the results of

B2B Customer Insight: The Proven Path to Growth, pp. 1–13
Copyright © 2012 by Information Age Publishing
All rights of reproduction in any form reserved.

the survey, I glanced over at the CEO to make sure he understood the implications of what I was saying.

Well, from what I could see, evidently he was either exerting a tremendous amount of concentration on my words … or he was sound asleep.

A moment later, a brief snore confirmed that the latter was the case.

I also suddenly realized that everyone else in the room was aware that the CEO was grabbing a catnap—instead of listening to information that would be vital to his company's future. And not just the company's future —the future of everyone who worked there as well, including the people that were in the room. Despite what was at stake for them, however, no one would dare wake the top executive up or acknowledge that anything was amiss.

No, everyone pretended nothing was happening and everyone, except the sleeping CEO, continued to listen attentively.

Now, I do not regard myself as the most mesmerizing person on earth, but I have done enough successful presentations to know that I am not usually guilty of acting as an Ambien substitute. That is why I knew I needed to know just what went wrong in this particular case. So, a few days after the meeting, I called my primary contact at the company and asked him why in the world the CEO had commissioned a customer insight survey that he did not intend to actually listen to.

The answer? The CEO had found out that the company he saw as the leader in the industry—his personal benchmark—had recently had a customer insight survey completed. He thought, to cover himself, he should have his own. Just a matter of keeping up with the Joneses.

Well, he did not keep up. As a matter of fact, his company is now out of business. And the other executives in that room lost hundreds of thousands of dollars when most of their pension fund disappeared.

What happened during that meeting was a sure sign that this firm was headed for a bad fall—a sure sign, and a comically obvious one. Those exact same dynamics, however, are at work in much subtler ways in every other company that is in the midst of sabotaging its own success. Bad decisions are made, necessary action is not taken (or unnecessary action is), warning signs are ignored, and those employees who are smart and alert enough to know things are going wrong are either encouraged to keep quiet or not listened to if they dare speak. The leadership is asleep at the wheel.

There are two primary ways this kind of mismanagement materializes—and we will define those ways a little later in this chapter. Just know, at this juncture, that although the reasons some companies fail and some succeed may seem vague and mysterious, they are actually fairly simple to pinpoint.

The harsh truth is that management can be asleep with their eyes wide open—because they are unwilling to wake up to the brutal realities of changing marketplaces. And, make no mistake about it, every marketplace is constantly changing—whether you are selling agricultural commodities, consumer electronics, heavy equipment or professional services.

That reality requires your business to wake up. As a wise man once said, "Recognize the need for change and make it while you still have a chance." That man is still with us—and his name is Bill Gates. His recognition of the need to change not only created a supremely successful company, but changed the way we all communicate and conduct business.

Change for its own sake is just fluff, window dressing. Unfortunately, many leaders confuse change with genuine strategy. Change without direction is just rearranging the deck chairs on the Titanic—but how many times have you heard or read statements like, "We have made this acquisition signaling a change in the way we do business," or "Our new organizational structure reflects our new philosophy." That is organizational doublespeak for saying, "We needed to change something, anything, so our investors will think we are actually spending their money wisely."

In contrast, change *with direction*, is evidence of strategic thinking. And that direction must derive from understanding what your customers want —how best to reach them—and how their tastes (and the marketplace) are changing. It is kind of like a person making sure they know where to get food and shelter—it is a matter of survival.

But in truth, companies need to do more than just survive. They need to *grow*.

THE IMPORTANCE OF GROWTH

That heading title seems self-evident, right? Of course, a business owner wants to generate as much revenue as he or she can, which will, hopefully, lead to higher profit. Moreover, our capitalistic system practically demands growth. The objective is always to make more money—especially since companies typically invest *ahead* of growth, in terms of supplies, equipment, facilities, personnel and so forth.

When that investment fails to pay off, when growth does not occur, the beginnings of a death spiral quickly become apparent. Low growth means that rising costs eat into constant levels of revenue and that profits decline. Less profit means less capital available to reinvest, which, in turn, means less product innovation and expansion. Generally, the operation continues to contract, unless the company is bought or infused with more outside cash in an attempt to keep it operating.

Growth, however, is not just important for the above reasons. In fact, I would argue, that financial considerations are the *second* most important reason that a company should keep expanding.

The most important reason? Growth keeps the company culture energized.

Yes, it is an intangible, but it is a critical intangible. Growth creates jobs, generates excitement, and confirms the vision and the passion with which the company was created in the first place. When a company is on the upswing, it gives everyone in the organization a sense and an understanding that the company has merit and worth. Everyone loves being part of a winning operation—it creates an overall affirmative mindset. That mindset causes employees to believe they can make things happen—and they generally do.

On the other hand, a company that is struggling for growth can make you feel as if you are attending a funeral that is only lacking a corpse. The difference is like night and day—I know, because I have seen it for myself. I am sure you have seen the same contrast. I will go into a meeting and be met with a "what is the use" attitude that instantly negates any constructive advice and reachable goals we are ready to provide. The management seems to be going through the motions, because they feel obligated to try and do *something*—but the real motivation to turn things around left the building a long time before we entered it.

For example, I recently met with a large professional association. Most of the top jobs at this association were clearly the result of entitlements, not merit, and the underlying profession was one that virtually guaranteed a very comfortable income. The elephant in the room was a looming, very large and obvious approaching threat to that income stream. This time, no one actually fell asleep during my presentation—but I could also could not see, feel or hear any sense of urgency about dealing with a troubling outlook.

And let us face it, for almost any business operating today, there are plenty of reasons to be concerned about the future. Information is widely shared and available, causing competition to be even fiercer to the point of being cutthroat, and to come from a wider geography. At the same time, because of the difficult economy, customers are trying every way imaginable to limit any price increases. The competitive base keeps growing and provides cheaper alternatives to domestic products. And mature industries in this country suddenly find themselves competing against every other country in the world—most of which have fewer costly regulations, flexible or illegal trade policies and much cheaper labor pools.

These challenges, however, can be met and overcome. That is the service we provide to our clients; researching and recommending alternative paths to maintain profitability. As an outside voice, however, we can only do so much. Company management is obviously behind the wheel and must steer the business in the correct direction. That the company ends up not on the road to success, but, instead, stuck in a ditch by the side of that road, is mainly due to three distinct problems with that management.

THE STRATEGY/EXECUTION MATRIX

I would like you to take a good look at the diagram below. It holds the keys to both good management—and bad.

As this matrix conveys, strategy and execution are the primary axis of a company's success; developing the right combination of them is the formula for growth. This is a more formal development of our discussion above where we used the terms "strategy" and "direction." You will see that positive outcome in the upper left quadrant that reads "Sustainable Value." Clearly, this is where every business wants to be—it results in long-term growth that keeps a company healthy in every important way.

When it comes to strategy and execution, balance is crucial. Favoring one over the other tilts the operation in ways that can topple the entire

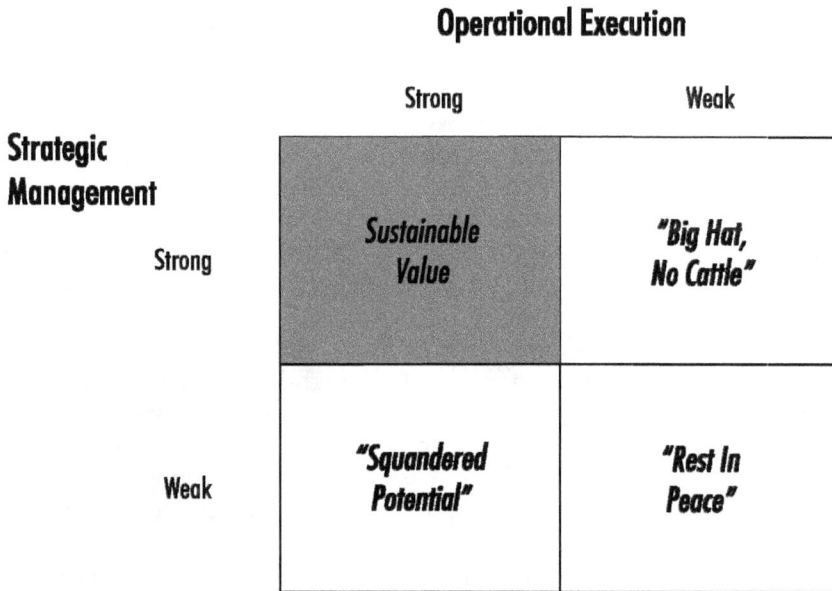

Operational Execution

	Strong	Weak
Strategic Management Strong	Sustainable Value	"Big Hat, No Cattle"
Weak	"Squandered Potential"	"Rest In Peace"

Figure 1.1.   Sustainable Value—where every business wants to be.

enterprise if left unchecked. At the very least, this imbalance will impede growth.

The first two of our three "Threats to Growth" concern these imbalances and their consequences.

THREAT TO GROWTH #1: STRONG STRATEGY, WEAK EXECUTION

There is a popular expression to describe a company that focuses on strategic management without giving proper weight to thinking through the operational execution of that strategy—"Big Hat, No Cattle" (it is even the title of a Randy Newman song). The term refers to someone who acts as if they are the biggest thing going, even though they actually have very little going for them. If you look at the upper right quadrant of the matrix, you will see where this particular dysfunction falls.

Acquisitions can be a major culprit in this arena. When a company is cash rich, it becomes like an overeager bidder at an auction, spending foolishly and not really thinking about whether he can use what he is buying. The business will say that buying another company will provide incredible synergy, as well as adding marketing and operational firepower —and then, after they make this heavily hyped purchase, they will end up with a disaster on their hands. After the fanfare surrounding the acquisition, the fire-sale disposition of the remaining assets a few years later happens quickly and quietly.

Announcing a constant stream of new products, new markets and new acquisitions may look good in press releases in which the CEO can brag about all of his or her wonderful plans—or in wonderful, colorful charts and PowerPoint presentations to analysts and investors. But, in reality, few of these over ambitious projects ever gets the follow-through attention it needs to succeed. In the meantime, the company's resources are spread too thin while attempting to do too many things at once, taking away vital focus on the core business.

Harvard Business School Professor Michael Porter once studied the acquisition history over 3 decades of 33 high-level companies that all resided in the top half of the Fortune 500. The results of that study were not encouraging to those that like to embark on buying binges. Companies who made acquisitions whose businesses were related to the buyers' ended up divesting 50 to 60% of those acquisitions because the fit did not work. That is over half.

The failure rate of acquisitions with a nonrelated business was even more startling—74%. Another study done by the McKinsey and Co. consulting group found that 61% of *all* acquisitions were ultimately money losers and not worth the purchase price.

Even when you think you have done your homework on the company you are after and the acquisition should be a no-brainer, you can still get burnt. Another anonymous case study (and I promise, this chapter will be the only one where we do not name names): one of our clients made a strategic decision to buy another company. On paper, it looked like an incredibly good fit and the acquisition, at the time, was doing quite well; so well, in fact, that the buyer decided to let the company continue to operate as autonomously as possible. The thinking was, why mess with success?

Well, in this case, some serious messing should have been done. The newly acquired company ended up losing 40% of their sales and heading south fast; they knew the dip was coming, they artificially boosted their sales through discounts and other short-term devices, and made them-selves look a lot better on paper than they actually were, so they would be a prime takeover target.

As a side note, it is almost never a good idea to let a new acquisition continue to operate as it did before the takeover. Without real synergy an acquisition cannot be financially justified and should never happen in the first place. But how can the synergy be realized without change to the acquired business? The acquiring company should put their stamp on the acquisition immediately by putting their own people and processes into place. This is no time for acquiescing to emotional pleas to preserve cul-ture. After all, who is buying whom? Even well run holding companies bring in proven systems to drive efficiency and improve profitability.

A relentless focus on improvement is an approach that one company has done almost to perfection. Milliken, one of the largest privately held companies in the country, built up an outstanding textile manufacturing brand since its beginnings in 1865. They, however, saw that textile manu-facturing in this country was no longer going to enable them to grow and thrive—so, they expanded their offerings to include carpet and chemical products that have proven very successful.

So what is the difference between Milliken and other textile companies that have either failed or are struggling to survive? Leadership. Roger Milliken, the head of the company, who took over the top seat in 1947 from his father, invested heavily in research and development, while many other textile companies (that are no longer in business) did not. He did not believe in a comfort zone.

Here is what his son, Roger Jr., has to say about his dad, in a 2009 arti-cle from *The Greenville Journal*, a weekly newspaper distributed in Spartan-burg, South Carolina, where the company, and the family, is located:

He hates complacency. He is a ferocious competitor, whether it is ping-pong or golf or anything. He does not do things in a light way. *He never has been interested in doing today what he did yesterday.* He had this saying that the biggest room in the world is the room for improvement.

—Roger Milliken, Jr.
The Greenville Journal, 2009

The italics in the above quote are mine, because, to me, it is the key phrase that sums up Milliken's ongoing success. Forget about yesterday, tomorrow's going to be different—so we have to be different too.

Milliken's reinvention, by the way, was not apparently done at the expense of their employees either. For 5 years running, *Fortune* magazine has named them as one of the 100 top companies to work for. Milliken proves that it is possible to buck today's global competition and maintain high standards at the same time.

THREAT TO GROWTH #2: STRONG EXECUTION, WEAK STRATEGY

When a bottle rocket goes off, it can make an impressive display. Unfortunately, it shoots every which way without any lasting impact. A business that has poor strategic management but excellent operational execution is much like that bottle rocket—it looks great to the untrained eye, but it is razzle dazzle is soon spent and all that is left is smoke slowly dissipating in the air.

This type of managerial dysfunction falls into the lower left quadrant of the matrix—what I like to call "squandered potential." A company in this quadrant knows how to execute, change direction and make things happen. Unfortunately, it may change direction as often as somebody might change their socks—and it also may make so many different things happen at once that it can not keep track of any of them.

Picture a company here in the developed world that excels at manufacturing their product. This company continues to focus on modernizing their plants, buying more expensive machinery, putting in statistical process control (SPC) to monitor quality and basically, putting all their resources into their manufacturing. And they are amazing at it, they can make any of their products in the most efficient and modern manner.

Unfortunately, with the rise of manufacturing capabilities in low labor regions of the world like Southeast Asia, their strategy is completely off the mark. Simply put, they can not possibly *outinvest cheap labor*. They may invest in a $250,000 piece of machinery that would eliminate two positions from the production line, but what good is that if they have to compete with two-dollar-a-day workers? Streamlining and automating only gets you so far; you still need the people and they are going to want a lot more in an hour than foreign employees will make in a day. This is not a political statement, it is just plain fact.

Now the actual measured quality of the company's products may be better in the sense that they have tighter tolerances and are made from superior raw material. And it is certainly a viable marketing strategy to impress upon consumers here that their output is "high quality." But those factors only work to a point; the incredibly low prices that overseas manufacturing provides on a routine basis can make it impossible *not* to choose their goods over American ones. That means the company faces a very bleak future if they can not develop a clear understanding of their customer's value equation.

Think about the cost of everything you buy today versus 25 years ago. You would probably say everything is a lot more expensive today than it was in 1987. That is not true of many manufactured goods, especially apparel. The cost of a dress shirt, for example, has declined dramatically in inflation-adjusted terms over the last few decades—because of the low cost of making them overseas. American designers are still making their margins, but the US manufacturing side of the business is virtually dead and buried for all but a few specialty brands.

So why would a company continue to focus on manufacturing when the writing has been on the wall for quite some time? Why would they spend time on a strategy that just leads to a dead end?

Simple. They are unwilling to leave their comfort zone. Doing what they have always done is convenient. It is what they know how to do and, up until now, it is what is worked for them. Frankly, they do not know how to do things any differently—and that is not a crime. What *is* a crime is not putting resources into rethinking the company's vision and creating products that will continue to be economically viable.

Imagine a comedian who keeps doing the same tired jokes long after they stopped being funny. He is still trying to get away with, "Take my wife —please." He gets less and less laughs, less and less people come to his shows and, finally, it hits him in the wallet; he gets fewer and fewer book-ings. The kicker is he does not look at himself and what he is doing to cre-ate these increasingly difficult career circumstances. Instead, he blames the audiences for not "getting" him. For not having a sense of humor. For not appreciating his "talent."

After awhile, it should become glaringly obvious that he can not blame the people he is supposed to be entertaining for not being entertained by him. When you are no longer delivering something people want, it is not their fault, it is yours. Obviously, the solution for this particular performer is to freshen up his act.

And that is exactly the same process that would have saved the all too real example of the manufacturing company we looked at earlier. By "freshening up" their approach, and researching what products they could produce with their enormous resources that *would* still be competitive, the company could take their proven ability to execute and combine it with a strategy that would ensure long-term survival.

The real fatal flaw of the Weak Strategy/Strong Execution quadrant is when a company is intent on taking as much action as possible without any real coherent vision behind it. A company is only capable of carrying through two or, at the most, three big mandates at a time. If management is trying to introduce a completely new product line *and* launching a major safety effort in its operation *and* pursuing an aggressive acquisition drive *and* taking the company public … well, something is going to give.

It all comes down to human nature. Multitasking computers and smart phones may make us think we are also capable of running 30 mental programs of our own at one time, but research says just the opposite. It is literally impossible to pay conscious attention to more than one thing at a time, according to Harvard Medical School researchers. When you think you are multitasking, you are actually just doing several tasks sequentially in rapid succession. And every time you switch gears, your brain has to "reboot"—and refocus on the new task. "Each time you have this alternation, there is a period in which you will make no progress on either task," says David Meyer, PhD, director of the Brain, Cognition, and Action Lab at the University of Michigan. "It is mental dead time."

Management can put in place policies that unintentionally scatter the company and send its people off in conflicting directions. This can really come to a head in the sales force. Salespeople are obviously going to be commission driven—the question becomes, what are those commissions based on? Is it new customers? Growth with existing customers? Profit margin? Sales of a certain product line? Because whatever those commission are linked to is going to determine where those salespeople focus their efforts—and what the company ends up selling. Even if it may not be what the company wants to focus on at the moment.

The fact is that people will pursue whatever personally rewards them. You can lay down policy and send out all the memos in the world backing up that policy, but all of it will be ignored if there is a different mechanism —formal or informal—in place for the salesperson to make more money. When you make those commission decisions, you are really dictating *behavior* at the company—behavior that is almost impossible to shake. Because they are going to follow the money.

This can even happen at the plant level. If bonuses are dependent on productivity, and you have set up a major safety initiative that ends up slowing down workers, you have pitted two major forces against each other. You can not expect two mandates to succeed if they can not happily coexist.

THREAT TO GROWTH #3: INEPTNESS

Okay, this final threat has nothing to do at all with any matrixes or quadrants. And it has everything to do with, forgive my bluntness, just being plain stupid. There is not a lot of excuse for what happens in this arena.

Here is another anonymous case study: we did work for a company that actually thought it was a good idea for everyone to take a 15-minute smoke break. Nothing wrong with that. Except the policy was to take that fifteen minute break *every single hour.*

That is 25% of each and every work day, willfully evaporated by management. Words almost failed me when I heard about this, but then, finally, a few managed to work their way to the front of my brain—words like, "crazy," "ludicrous" and "suicidal."

Other forms of ineptness are more easily understood; for example, when a company misreads what they should be selling and to whom. This is a wrong turn that happens on a regular basis. A lot of the info about the marketplace comes from the sales force—but, as we just discussed in the last section of this chapter, that sales force can be incredibly biased toward their own self-interest, which does not necessarily match up with the company's best interests.

Even the dynamics of a management meeting can alter the perception of the market in a negative way. Whoever argues the loudest or most eloquently can easily dominate an important discussion and cause the wrong decision to be made. Or someone may have just read an article in *The Wall Street Journal* that motivates a sudden inexplicable push for a major company policy revision, even though the current policy may be what serves the company the best.

And frankly that kind of anecdotal evidence—a newspaper article, a TV report or even a stray remark by a business associate—is frequently the basis for really wrong headed decisions. In these cases, company management does not take the time to do the necessary research to make an informed decision. In one case I remember, our client's management suddenly ordered a plant manager to reconfigure everything in order to make a new product. That came about because the CEO happened to be walking through the production facility of another firm that used them as a supplier and overheard someone say they needed a certain particular product. Based on that random remark, and on nothing else, my client was suddenly going to a lot of time and expense to supply this product.

The other side of that same coin is that you can receive good data and completely misread it. The challenge is always separating true change from random noise.

A company might interpret a short-term growth in sales and see it as a trend—when, in reality, it is a blip. Another company might manufacture products meant for elderly consumers, see that the number of elderly people is growing rapidly and assume they have made a wise decision— when, in reality, they have not done their homework and a new advance in technology is about to make their products obsolete.

There is never just *one* question to be answered—there are dozens. When we prepare a report for our clients, our mandate is to look at their challenges from every perspective. Good news should be challenged, bad news should be analyzed for the upside and future projections should be bounded by all appropriate considerations.

Finally, I would like to talk about the catastrophe of success. Companies that maybe are not really all that good can still be incredibly lucky—and develop a momentum that seems unstoppable. Invariably, these companies become complacent—they do not develop new products, but keep making a whole lot of money. And that money colors everything.

It also invariably causes decisions to be made that threaten that cash-rich status. In the for-profit world, private equity owners, analysts and stockholders all pressure companies sitting on piles of capital to invest, even though there might not be any immediate available investment that makes a lot of sense.

Before the 2008 recession hit, for instance, when money was plentiful, many companies were facing that kind of investment pressure. In a manufacturing or distribution segment, an attractive price to pay for an acquisition may be a multiple of five or six times its EBITDA (earnings before interest, tax, depreciation and amortization). Suddenly, companies with fat bank accounts were willing to pay up to eight or nine times the EBITDA—a display of crazy spending with almost no hope of a good return. It is how bubbles are created and common sense is left at the curb. And, of course, we know how the last bubble popped in the closing months of 2008.

Outside pressures. Inside whims. Impulsive actions. Ignorance or misreading of the market. The common denominator to the above factors, all of which more often than not lead to disastrous decisions, is a lack of thinking things through. Business, like any other endeavor on planet earth, can be helped or harmed by the unexpected—but ongoing mismanagement creates a certain formula for failure down the line.

In this chapter, I have talked about the specifics of why some companies fail to grow. Not that failure is a hard thing to pull off—it is as easy as missing a baseball when you are up at bat. Knocking that same ball out of the park is a whole other story. That is because success, of course, is always the more impressive and elusive achievement—one that requires not just hard work and effort, but also, as we have seen, informed strategy and strong execution.

The "informed" part of the equation is critical—and that is what the rest of this book is all about. My company, Priority Metrics Group, Inc., (PMG) has as its mandate to identify and capture growth opportunities for our clients. We do that by providing tailored B2B customer insight surveys that go beyond the norm to provide suppliers with the exact information they need to take advantage of those opportunities.

Again, this seems like common sense—when you know the most you possibly can about who is buying what you are selling, you are able to make the kind of knowledgeable decisions that pay off down the line. The fact of the matter is, our 18 years of experience have taught us that you have to ask the right questions of the right people, then frame the data in the exact right way in order for this kind of survey to really be of benefit to a business.

The good news is we have developed an effective and unique methodology to do just that for B2B companies. The clients that have taken advantage of what we have discovered in our research have enjoyed many large market advantages—and have also avoided unnecessary potential disasters that we have pointed out to them. To their credit, they listened to what their customers had to say and reacted to it in a timely and motivated fashion. In other words … they did not fall asleep at our presentation!

You will be hearing from many of those clients in the chapters to come; they have been kind enough to allow me to share their compelling stories in this book. You will also find out the secrets of how our customer insight surveys are designed, implemented and applies, and how they enable a company to not only determine new and viable prospects for growth, but also successfully take advantage of them. That is because we insist on providing practical advice our clients can realistically put into action, rather than untethered research that does not lead to proactive conclusions.

In this chapter, I have discussed what prevents growth. In the next chapter, I will look at what helps a B2B company achieve significant and sustainable growth—simply by delivering what their customers want.

But first, they have to *understand* what they want.

CHAPTER 2

VALUE

The Engine of Growth

We probably would not be here if it were not for the automotive business.
—Hal Bates
Market Manager of Technical Fabrics
Glen Raven, Inc.

GLEN RAVEN CASE STUDY: THE NECESSITY FOR A NEW MARKET

In 1999, Glen Raven was a company at the crossroads. Much of the market for the product they currently manufactured was rapidly being taken over by overseas factories at a price Glen Raven simply could not compete with, due to incredibly low labor costs. Their only choice was to find a new market that required their supplier to make their product in the United States.

They looked around and came to the conclusion that their salvation was located in Detroit. If they could gain entry to the auto industry, that could be the ticket to long-range profitability. Glen Raven, however, had few connections to this industry and no way to know if they actually had any chance at ultimately gaining entry to what was a very exclusive group of suppliers.

B2B Customer Insight: The Proven Path to Growth, pp. 15–27
Copyright © 2012 by Information Age Publishing
All rights of reproduction in any form reserved.

That is when they turned to us at Priority Metrics Group. Our job was to talk to Ford, General Motors (GM), Toyota, Honda and other original equipment manufacturers to see what they required from a supplier, if there was room for another supplier and if they would consider a company like Glen Raven as that supplier. We intended to do that through our customer insight survey process.

Easier said than done. Companies like Ford are far from an easy wall to breach. Operators will not tell you who is in charge of what—and will not transfer you through to an extension unless you know the other party's full name. Of course, you can not get that full name unless you talk to someone in the specific department first—and, of course, you can not talk to someone in that specific department without a full name. It is the researcher's Catch-22—but, after over 400 phone calls, we finally found our way through the system and were successful in tracking down the right power players.

The challenge did not stop with getting the right names, however. The customer insight survey needed to uncover how Glen Raven could deliver unique value to the car companies. Their needs were already being met by their current suppliers—which meant another one trying to get in the door had to demonstrate they could deliver *more* value than the companies that are already selling to them.

The good news is that General Motors (GM) *was* open to a new supplier—it was in their best interests to have multiple suppliers as a back-up in case some unforeseen circumstances prevented one from delivering. But a new supplier had to have the right credentials. Since we positioned Glen Raven as an established global and financially secure manufacturer (which, of course, they were) when we discussed their possibilities with the car company, that hurdle was easy to get over.

The next hurdle, however, proved to be a long and expensive one. Glen Raven had to develop their manufacturing process with GM over the next 3 years and make a significant investment of time, resources and money, before they received any large orders from the car maker.

The happy result, however, was that today Glen Raven supplies 40% of GM's headliner fabric—an important and ongoing profit center for the company that had been looking for a new one. In the words of Hal Bates, Market Manager of Technical Fabrics at Glen Raven, "We would not be here if it were not for the automotive business. We started from zero when we contacted PMG. They probably did not charge us enough."

We appreciate Hal's kind words, but our customer insight survey only provides the roadmap to achieving business goals. Many times, that roadmap is completely ignored, even though it is completely focused on how to help the company in question achieve substantial and significant growth—an objective you would not think *could* be ignored. But, if you have read the last chapter, you understand how that can happen at a company.

Glen Raven, to their credit, took huge risks in following our particular roadmap for them. Those risks fortunately paid off in enormous ways. And beyond following our roadmap, Glen Raven also stepped up and provided a unique fabric blend that would make GM's vehicles more attractive to consumers. They added value to the business equation that made GM and others stand up and take notice.

THE POWER OF VALUE

The important takeaway from this case study is that the most significant steps Glen Raven took to secure GM's business were about *value*, not cost. Haggling over price was certainly a part of this long-term negotiation, but raising GM's comfort level regarding working with Glen Raven as a company, was critical.

Whereas impediments to growth frequently spring from *internal* mismanagement, the spurs for growth come from analyzing and meeting the all-important *external* needs of the marketplace, i.e. the customer. Our customer insight survey did just that for Glen Raven, and allowed them to pursue the value increases that would make the difference.

Many businesses make the mistake of assuming that *price is the only thing that matters* when it comes to making a sale. Do not get me wrong, it is certainly important. But there is a concept that is even more important that price—and that is *value*. Value sets the stage for long-term company growth far more than price ever can.

For the purposes of this discussion, let is define "value" as the total benefit of product and service translated into economic worth, as seen in Figure 2.1.

People buy based on what the best deal is—what they are getting versus what they are paying. All things being equal, the customer, yes, is going to buy on price. But, the truth is, all things are almost *never* equal—there are differences in dimensions, adherence to customer specifications, product appearance, raw material, finish, features and functionality, and performance. And there are always differences between suppliers, differences that can be exploited.

Those differences can take the form of tech support, extended warranties, superior customer service, ongoing product development efforts that continually improve what you can provide, and so forth.

Even if you are talking about two suppliers who sell the exact same product, they are not going to supply the same overall *value*. Every sup-

Value:

the total benefit of product and associated service translated into economic worth

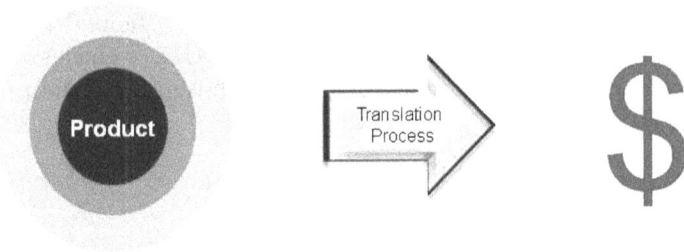

Figure 2.1.   Value is defined by the customer.

plier brings *unique value attributes* to the table—and those value attributes *can be sold at a higher price*.

UNDERSTANDING VALUE ATTRIBUTES

There are three main categories of features or attributes which a business can use to create value for their customers.

Price/Cost Value

Price/Cost Value includes, obviously, the cost of the product, but also includes payment terms, transactions costs and other elements. When people think about value, they typically (and very quickly) associate this particular aspect with it. However, value also includes many nonprice attributes as well.

Performance Value

Performance Value is one of those nonprice attributes. You may supply the cheapest widget in the world, but if that widget breaks after three uses, you are not supplying a high level of value. If the product does not perform as advertised, or if it performs well, but not the way the customer wanted or expected, the performance value is reduced. This attribute also includes product delivery as well as service and support.

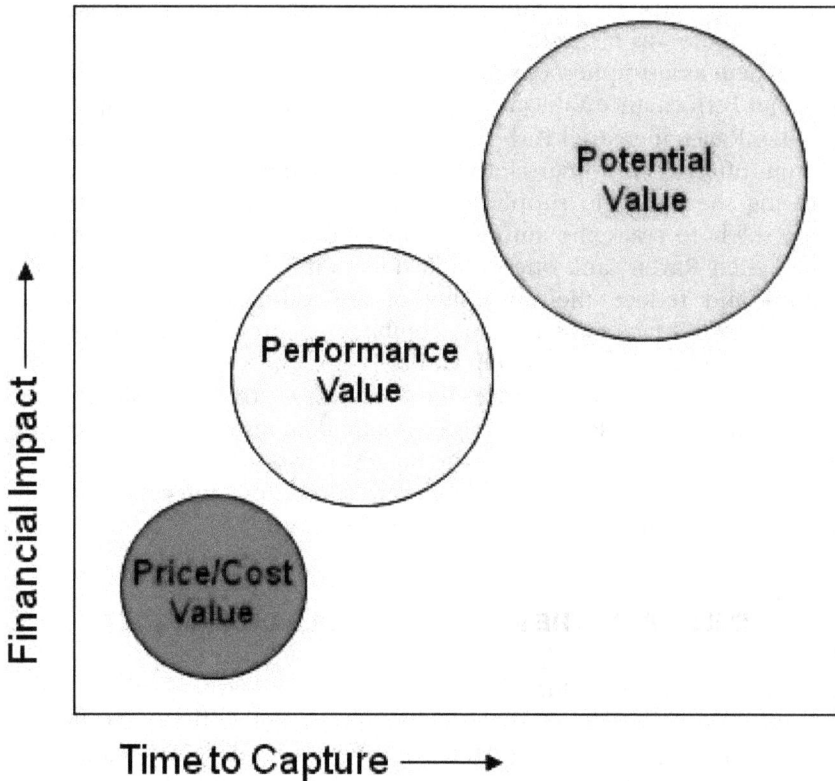

Figure 2.2.   The dimensions of value.

Potential Value

The other nonprice value attribute has to do with Potential Value. The customer may benefit from a supplier that possesses a broad product line, for example, or one that has a high-level image or reputation. A supplier may also have access to new markets, due to their plant locations or market knowledge that could benefit the customer. These benefits offer the customer potential value that will require some further action or investment to fully exploit.

The difficulty in convincing a customer to pay a higher price for the latter two categories of nonprice value attributes can be considerable. But the fact is, especially when it comes to B2B sales, *those particular attributes actually provide the highest potential gain to the customer.* The customer has to be made aware of that potential gain, and understand how it benefits them.

Let us go back to the Glen Raven case study. Again, the Price/Cost value attribute was far from the biggest factor involved in GM's decision to use them as a supplier. Certainly, Glen Raven's price had to be competitive, but Performance Value and Potential Value were far more important.

Glen Raven increased Performance Value by hiring a sales rep based in Detroit, offering headliner cloth with superior performance capabilities, ensuring the ability to supply long-term, and many other investments made solely to crack the automotive market. When it came to Potential Value, Glen Raven sank one million dollars into a lab to insure quality control and reduce the possibility of any off-quality product being shipped to the factory. The value combination provided a unique cost-effective product that would help GM sell cars.

If you take a look at the above chart, you will see the larger significance of Performance and Potential Value visually demonstrated—and you will also see that Potential Value has the biggest pay-off for the customer, but takes the longest time for the customer to successfully interpret and capture in their business.

DELIVERING THE PERFECT "BUNDLE OF BENEFITS"

We have verified this value phenomenon repeatedly with our research—time after time, we have heard customers comment that they are willing to pay a premium price for suppliers with superior product knowledge, customer service, long-term stability and other facets unrelated to actual product cost. A supplier investing in these "intangibles" may not immediately profit from them but will, down the line, realize more revenues and discover new business opportunities because of them. And the amazing fact is that, in many cases, the additional customer value is created with no incremental cost of production or delivery.

That is because of an important change of perspective. The supplier stops looking at what they sell as simply the product itself, and starts looking at all the intangibles they can provide *with* that product—what some marketers call a "bundle of benefits." The tangible and intangible elements of the product are benefits only to the customer—that is why the change of perspective is critical. The supplier usually can not see the same elements as benefits. To the supplier, they are just things—extra costs, added hassle, more time, a change in the way they do business. These types of auxiliary benefits fall mostly into the Performance and Potential Value categories.

To give you a consumer-based example, when a cell phone service provider sells you a phone, it is *not* just selling you that phone. It is selling you its monthly plan of minutes, internet features on the phone, available games, ringtones, the camera that is in the phone, and the warranty on the phone, among other things.

The same thing goes for B2B transactions, as the Glen Raven example makes clear. Even a sales rep can be part of that "bundle of benefits." If the rep has a great relationship with the customer, if that person demonstrates a good understanding of the customer's business, that is worth money to them. If the rep can help with credit terms and solve delivery problems, that also adds important value. Whatever way you can bring increase to your side of the equation, you add value to your product.

A benefit to the customer can even be something as simple as a supplier's location. If you are physically closer to the customer than other suppliers, that is probably a big benefit to them. Going back to a consumer example, there are thousands of Subway sandwich franchises across the country—and they all provide the same basic food choices, one is not going to be markedly better than the other. But obviously, you are going to eat at the one that is across the street, because it is the most convenient. Similarly, you may sell corrugated boxes, the same boxes as a thousand other suppliers, but you might be able to sell yours to a buyer just because your facility is closest.

Once you realize that certain aspects of your business can be more important to your future growth than the products you actually sell, the next question becomes which value attributes do you focus on to achieve real growth?

GOING BEYOND PRICE: VALUE DETERMINATION

Deciding which value attributes to focus on means you must understand how your customers determine which attributes are most important to *them*. Understanding how a buyer in a B2B transaction makes a value determination, however, can be very difficult. It differs markedly from how a consumer makes their buying decision.

For example, when a consumer is trying to decide which brand of toothpaste to purchase, it is usually just up to that consumer. Does he or she want the reassurance of a big name brand, the cost benefit of a generic or store brand, or the premium expense of toothpaste with an extra feature, such as whitening or plaque prevention?

The final decision is either a default one (he or she buys the same kind of toothpaste they always buy) or it is made on the fly while cruising down the aisle of the store, informed possibly by advertising exposure as well as personal preferences. And if that one consumer rejects a certain brand of toothpaste, the manufacturer never really knows about it and does not really care—unless, of course, a huge chunk of consumers begin rejecting the brand over time. That always seems to get a company's attention!

When a buyer makes a value determination in the B2B world, however, it is almost never an individual decision. Instead, it is a complex verdict that involves a number of people—it could be five, six or even fifteen people involved in the buying decision. Those people require a substantial amount of information about the product, the supplier, the channel of distribution, the raw materials used in manufacture and the suppliers of those raw materials, and on and on. Once the specifications are set and the potential suppliers of products that meet those specs are identified, the decision ostensibly comes down to price—who can supply that set of specs at the lowest cost.

Of course, that is hard on the sellers; they do not want to have to compete strictly on a price basis. And, the shocking fact is that *neither do the customers*—but it is difficult for a buyer to justify other factors beyond cost once the specs have been finalized, if, in fact, the products from all suppliers appear to have no point of difference. That message gets heard loud and clear by the supplier's sales reps, who will end up going back and telling the home office that making a deal needs to be all about charging the least amount of money.

And make no mistake, in this buying situation, there is a lot more pressure on a supplier selling to a business than a business selling to a consumer. If the supplier's bid is rejected, that company is looking at large amounts of dollars lost and, as a result, jobs, management and even infrastructure. When providing the lowest bid seems to be the easiest path to getting the business the supplier so desperately wants, that is the option that will frequently be chosen.

But that is *not* usually the case.

It is not really the sales rep's fault for focusing on price. He usually does not have the tools to effectively sell other value attributes—price is the easiest path to pursue. And it is not the buyer's fault for focusing on price—especially when no supplier is actually dealing with real value propositions. However, if the supplier can demonstrate they provide superior value in the areas that count, that supplier can win the deal—even though the price may be *higher* than the competition's.

But again, the supplier needs to know which value attributes are going to make the difference. All those people involved in the buying decision that we spoke of earlier all have *different needs*. For instance, the engineer involved does not particularly care about price, he cares about the product meeting all his technical criteria—without any worries on his end. The warehouse manager only cares that she can keep the necessary components and pieces in stock and can supply them quickly when needed. The marketing manager wants a product that adds value in the eyes of the end user—adding a feature that is demanded by the end user and, even better, different from competition.

Everyone has their own particular "wish list"—and many of those wishes have *nothing* to do with Price/Cost Value and have *everything* to do with our old friends, Performance Value and Potential Value.

Now imagine that, when all these people involved in the buying decision sat down at a meeting to decide on a supplier, you *could actually know* what each of them valued—and you also knew what the *relative importance* of each of those aspects was. That would enable you, as a supplier, to create a value proposition that would put you ahead of the pack not only in terms of what you were offering, but in terms of the price you could command—because you would be *supplying greater value attributes to all parties concerned* than the competition.

Well, of course, you can not know exactly what all the people in that meeting are actually thinking. A customer insight survey, however, gets you as close as you possibly can to having that ideal information. When done properly, customer insight will tell you what everyone who is in on the buying decision is looking for, what each of them value and what your competitive position is. With that information in hand, you can create a value proposition that works—delivering dollars to the buyer and potentially to the end users by allowing them to do more, do it in new ways, do it faster, and reduce costs.

CUSTOMER INSIGHT OBJECTIVES

Let us talk a little about just what a customer insight survey should accomplish for a company—at least as PMG uses it.

First of all, the survey should help the company understand how their customers perceive them as a supplier—and how they are perceived versus other suppliers being used. We also discover where the opportunities are for our client to increase their share with the customer— whether it is a case of expanding distribution or modifying existing products so they offer more value.

To break it down even further, here are the three main "bullet point" questions our customer insight survey will answer for our client:

- How is our client's performance compared to their customers' expectations?
- What is important to their customers and what are their priorities when it comes to suppliers?
- How is our client performing compared to their competition?

Answering those questions thoroughly with a proven unbiased methodology allows us to inform our clients of which value attributes are going to matter the most to their customers.

APPLYING ATTRIBUTES TO CUSTOMERS

Value is the engine that propels a company's growth—and there are only two avenues that company can travel down to achieve that growth: current customers and new customers. Obviously, a company's success depends on continually expanding their sales and market share—and that can only be done by either gaining a greater share of sales from existing customers or linking up with customers that have not bought from you before.

Let us take a look at both categories and see how value attributes come into play with each.

Current Customers

Your current customers are the base of your business—but they are also an often overlooked avenue of growth. Most businesses spend the bulk of their marketing efforts and promotional dollars on getting new customers. Meanwhile, your existing customers are a lot easier and definitely more cost effective to sell to. You already have a relationship with them and they presumably like buying from you—why should not you make the attempt to expand your share of their business? It is definitely less daunting than making a cold call on someone who really has no idea who you are.

The question is how do you make a serious run at making more money from the same customer? Your answer should come from what is revealed in a customer insight survey. In general, you have three options as to how you expand your share—either *sell more of what you currently sell, sell what you currently provide to them at a higher price* or *sell them products you have not sold to them before*.

The first two cases are actually very similar. You must provide more value that justifies that greater share or higher price. It is also incumbent upon you to educate the customer about why the increased share or higher price is better for them (a process that we will talk about shortly in this chapter).

To illustrate this concept, think about why you might pay a different price to send a package through the mail. If you want it to arrive faster, you pay more. If you want delivery confirmation, you pay more. If you want insurance on the value of the package, you pay more. All of these features have nothing to do with the physical act of getting that package from one place to another—they are all extra value attributes (that "bundle of benefits") that justify you paying a higher delivery charge.

Similarly, there may be value attributes you can add to your product or service that can motivate a customer to pay more for it. You do not add these added benefits blindly, because they may not be ones your customer particularly cares about, let alone is willing to stretch its budget for. Instead, you use the customer insight survey to identify these opportunities and then explain their usefulness to the business in question.

Customer insight can also suggest which additional products the customer might consider buying from the supplier, as well as the bundle of benefits those additional products would require to make the supplier's pitch the most attractive to the customer.

It should be noted that there are some inherent limitations to this strategy. When businesses sell to businesses, the customer will, in some cases, have restrictions in place as far as how much share they are allowed to give one supplier. These restrictions are usually created so that a business is not too dependent on any one supplier—and that, if something should happen to one, they still have others lined up that can successfully pick up the slack. Supply contracts may limit price increases to documented increases in raw material or other costs.

It all comes back to the old business maxim, "Just give the customers what they want." In order to do that, you have to find out *what* they want. The purpose of customer insight is just that—and, as a result, gives you the most realistic avenues to explore in terms of increasing market share with a customer. The survey "prepares the way" for this increase—and lets the supplier know just what the possibilities are and how to approach those possibilities.

New Customers

Understanding the needs of potential customers is a much bigger challenge. As we noted earlier, if there is no working relationship in place, finding the right people and getting your message heard is hard work. It is also much more difficult to answer the value questions that need to be posited—because even a third party company conducting the survey has to start "cold" with them.

And that last sentence right there provides the key to winning business from a new customer. That company has to see, and *believe*, that you can solve a problem for them. The problem can be one they know about, such as being dissatisfied with one or two of their current suppliers or wanting to line up additional ones—or a problem they do not know about, like being able to lower their costs or help them sell more of what they make. Otherwise, you are not bringing anything to table. Buyers only change suppliers when there is a good reason to—it is up to the suppliers to provide those reasons.

Sometimes the customer is not even aware of the power of the added value you can bring to their products. That is why the supplier must effectively educate that customer as to why and how they will benefit from doing business with them, especially if it is a benefit they had not considered before.

This is a process that consumer-based businesses do all the time through advertising. Did anyone really worry about getting their pizza in "30 Minutes or Less" before the nationwide pizza chain Dominos made it an integral part of their advertising? This was a benefit consumers did not really even consider—but suddenly it was one they wanted. Similarly, a supplier must educate new customers about benefits they may not know about—but will not want to do without once they know they are available.

Another challenge in capturing a new customer is a supplier must often make a large investment merely to be seriously considered as one of their suppliers, such as Glen Raven did with GM. With current customers, a supplier will have more confidence putting that kind of money into getting new business from them—the supplier already deals with them on a daily basis and can have more confidence in an expensive strategy that will expand their share. With a new customer, it is more of a roll of the dice —one that can be mitigated by customer insight, but still not a sure thing. A supplier needs to look carefully at how much it is going to cost to acquire that added business—and whether that added business will justify that investment.

For example, a supplier might have all of a customer's business for a certain product. But that customer may have other product lines that use material that the supplier makes—so it would be easy for both parties if the supplier provides that product as well. In order to create the necessary value to entice the customer to buy that additional product, the supplier might sustain significant extra costs in support, service and other areas of their operation. So the final question has to be—"Are we going to make money if we go after that extra business?"

If the supplier is not going to make its necessary profit margins on the new product, it may be more productive in the long run to walk away from attempting to grab that extra business, and leave the less profitable products to other suppliers. It is always important to run those numbers and not assume that selling other products to an existing customer is always going to be instantly profitable.

To sum up, yes, the overriding factor to providing growth is value. Value is not just about dollars and cents, as I hope I have made clear—it is

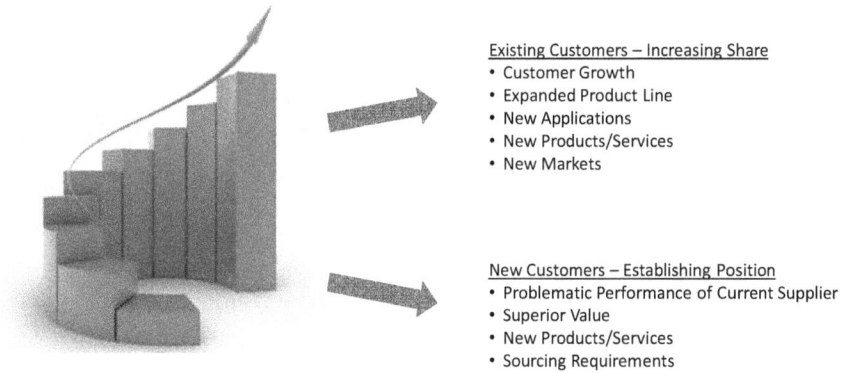

Existing Customers – Increasing Share
- Customer Growth
- Expanded Product Line
- New Applications
- New Products/Services
- New Markets

New Customers – Establishing Position
- Problematic Performance of Current Supplier
- Superior Value
- New Products/Services
- Sourcing Requirements

Figure 2.3.   An overview of how to leverage growth with existing and new customers.

also about perception and intangibles. At the end of the day, however, the cost of delivering that value should be carefully assessed on the supplier's end.

Leveraging value and effectively educating both new and current customers as to the importance of that value means more money and more growth. That process begins by learning how potential buyers make their value determinations.

In our next chapter, I will look at how we put a customer insight survey into motion to ensure that the best, most unbiased data is collected. If the first steps are not right, the survey itself will not be either.

CHAPTER 3

GAINING CUSTOMER INSIGHT

> The perspective on what is being said by customers is very important. It should be used to start a dialogue internally ... with feedback from all levels.
>
> —Matt Nyberg
> former VP Business Development
> Lincoln Industries

LINCOLN INDUSTRIES CASE STUDY: EXPECTATION VERSUS REALITY

Since 1993, Lincoln Industries, located in Lincoln, Nebraska, had used the same nationally known research firm to do an annual customer satisfaction survey. A few years ago, Matt Nyberg joined the company and believed that firm's methodology did not really serve Lincoln's particular needs. Since I already knew Matt, and he was familiar with and trusted PMG's processes, he asked us to begin providing an annual customer insight survey instead.

Lincoln had two primary groups of customers, which they serviced with two independent arms: (1) their core customers, also their biggest customers, which involved complex buying decisions, very long-term perspectives, a lot of technical development and relationship building at many different levels of those companies, and (2) their commercial customers, a broader and more diverse set of customers, who were transaction oriented. The word Lincoln constantly got back from their sales

B2B Customer Insight: The Proven Path to Growth, pp. 29–44
Copyright © 2012 by Information Age Publishing
All rights of reproduction in any form reserved.

force and others that dealt with the commercial customers was that the important factor in selling to this group was price, price, price.

The differences between the two groups were pretty black and white—that is why Lincoln expected the findings of the survey would also be clear-cut; the core customers would be concerned with Lincoln's more intangible value attributes (relationships, delivery performance, quality level, etc.) and the commercial customers would be reacting to the cost of Lincoln's product.

Well, the findings *were* that black and white—but to virtually everyone's surprise, in exactly the *opposite* way they had anticipated. The core customers were overwhelmingly concerned with Lincoln's prices—while the commercial customers were far less concerned with price than with other value provided by Lincoln as a company. Lincoln was so thrown by these results that they came back to us to double check that our findings were attached to the right groups.

They were. And once the company began reading the actual comments from the customers in question and had an internal dialogue about them, they realized why the survey had come out the way it had and what action should be taken.

"There was clearly more going on there that we thought," says Matt now. "It was easy to say that there was something wrong with the data. Fortunately, PMG came in and explained it. That prompted more discussion to help discover what was going on and what we had to do to follow up on it."

What Matt and the other Lincoln Industries executives discovered was that our findings were not quite as simple as they seemed. For example, on the commercial customer side, the reason there was so much concern over the overall value that Lincoln provided was that *they were not aware* of everything Lincoln as a company put into their product. The answer on that side was more about educating the commercial costumers about that value rather actually having to change up what they were already providing.

But Lincoln never would have known this was a critical factor to that group without gaining the proper customer insight—and without working toward the proper *interpretation* of that insight.

Now, this may surprise you, since our business is providing that kind of Customer insight to our clients, but, in this chapter, I am going to reveal just how companies can gain that insight on their own through their existing processes. It is not that this information is unavailable to a company; it is more a matter of mustering up the resources to focus on it and doing the necessary follow-through to gather it. So let us talk about the methods most companies already have in place to gain substantial customer insight on their own.

THE SALES FORCE FACTOR

First and foremost, a company's sale force is the prime source for information about their customers. You have got people there that are talking to customers every single day—hearing their complaints, their needs and even revealing possible future opportunities for increasing a supplier's market share.

Unfortunately, in most cases, that steady stream of valuable knowledge is left untapped. Simple facts that could strongly impact a supplier's future strategy are not communicated to the necessary decision makers.

The plain truth is that anybody who is serious about gaining an understanding of their company's customers needs to utilize the sales force. And an easy way to do that is to simply upgrade the comprehensiveness of the sales call reports that pretty much any salesperson has to file after calling on a customer.

Our experience is that, generally, these call reports just provide the basics to management—the company they met with, the specific representatives involved, the time and date of the meeting, the purpose and the outcome. The meat of them will provide the following kind of minimal summary:

> Met with Bill Williams, head of purchasing for ABC Company. He said ABC would need to buy by the end of the year and would like us to rebid on 7,000 units instead of 2,000. I informed him we would get him the new numbers by Thursday. Left him a pen and pencil set.

Read that over again—and then look at the following long list of important questions left unanswered by the Call Report:

- Why was the order increased?
- Who is the salesperson's company competing against for the order?
- Which person at the customer company will make the call as to who gets the order?
- How likely is ABC Company to buy from the salesperson's company?
- Is the salesperson doing anything beyond providing revised numbers to close the deal?
- Why is the order being delayed to the end of the year?

These are all very, very big questions that are important to the supplier—and the answers would probably initiate some significant action, or, at the very least, some vital account planning. But the answers are

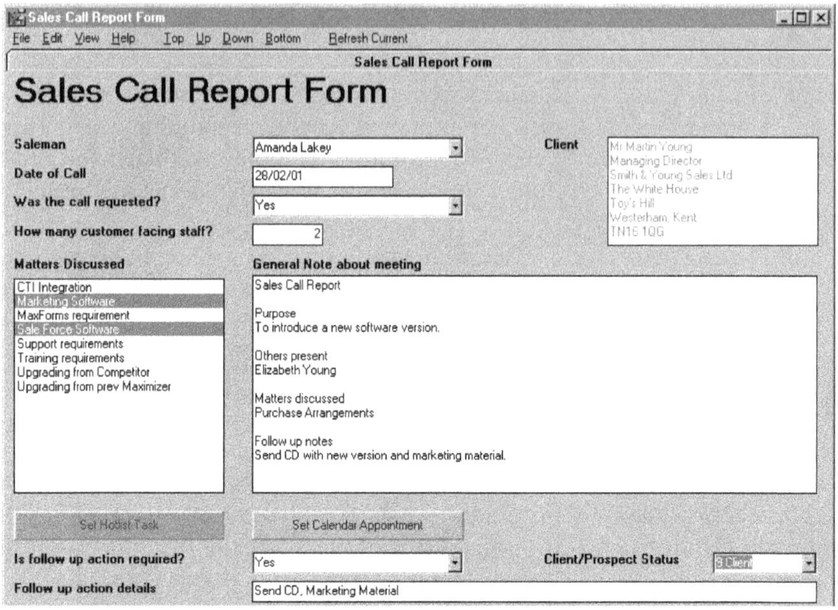

Figure 3.1.   Sample sales call report.

probably not going to come unless internal systems are changed to solicit them.

That is because the real purpose of these call reports is not to gather customer insight, but to keep an eye on the salesperson and make sure she is doing her job. If everything that was indicated on the call report represented the sole content of that sales meeting, it should have lasted about thirty seconds. You may get the "Who, What and Where"—but you will rarely if ever get the "Why" or the "How," which brings about the deeper insight into the customer's current and future plans that is essential to know.

And there is no question that this kind of information gets exchanged. During the traditional small talk that accompanies all these kinds of sales appointments, the customer may have talked about a new product line they are looking to launch down the line. Or perhaps a new plant they are about to build. These crucial bits of news, however, never get on the sales report, because they do not directly affect the salespeople and their jobs—and their compensation. They do not care and nobody ever gets the customer information that could be beneficial—or detrimental—to the supplier's future. The salespeople simply assume—and rightly so—that management uses these reports to keep their eye on them. Many just make up appointments to pad out their schedule and look busier than they actually are.

But it is not just the fault of the sales force. Only thoughtful companies look at call reports as a proactive tool to help bolster the supplier's future sales. What usually happens is that management scans the call reports and then, if the number of appointments does not add up to what they expect to see, they scold the salesperson and tell her she needs to make more calls—which, of course, is why the salespeople feel obligated to make more up as a preemptive strike. More substantial information is not encouraged and, therefore, is not given.

The way to solve this crucial problem is to give the salespeople an incentive to report this kind of information. It does not have to be financial; it could be that, if a need for a new product is flagged by the salesperson, he gets the sale, recognition at a company event, and perhaps an assistant or new iPad to help out with the new business. It is also vital to have someone in place who is responsible for compiling this information and putting it into the company's development report.

A call report template should call for more specific information—to ensure that it goes beyond the Dragnet "Just the facts, ma'am" mentality into a relevant analysis of what is going on, such as:

- Who are the decision makers on any upcoming sales?
- What issues have to be dealt with to close the sale?
- Who is competing for the order in question?
- When will the sale actually be concluded?
- What steps must the salesperson—and the supplier—take to make sure they get the order?

In addition, competitive intelligence can be made part of the equation, if it is not already. In many cases, a supplier's salespeople are signing in at a customer's office right after the competition's rep has been in to make a pitch. The customer may even comment to the salesperson about what the competing rep had to offer. The salesperson should report back on that kind of basic information, so management knows what other suppliers are in the mix on a bid, and how seriously they are being taken. When this kind of critical information is made a part of the call report, it can help the sales force close more deals and the help the company make more money. Is not that what everyone wants?

OTHER CUSTOMER INSIGHT PROCESS MECHANISMS

As with the sales call reports, there are other mechanisms that most companies have in place as standard operating procedure that can be used to gain customer insight—if an effort is made to actually compile and make use of the readily available information.

Let us run down a few examples of these routine processes and how they can used to gain meaningful customer insight:

QUALITY CONTROL DOCUMENTS

Most suppliers, when they ship an order, will insert a little card or some other documentation into that order that says they have verified the contents of the order on their end and want to make sure all is right on the customer's side. For example, a quality control card might say, "You have got the 42 widgets as ordered. We would like you to answer a few questions to make sure your order was processed as promised." There might follow a few questions such as, "Was the order delivered on time?" "Was everything in perfect condition or was anything damaged?" and so forth. There would also be room for the customer to comment about the order if need be.

This card is then meant to be sent back to the supplier, where it will usually make its way to the foreman of the shipping department. As with the call reports, the foreman will usually check to make sure that all went well with the delivery, and then throw the card into that particular customer's file—or worse, throw it out.

Again, the end result is another missed opportunity for customer insight. If someone would correlate the results from those cards, the company might find they have delivered 99% of their orders on time or without any problem at all—a fact they could brag about in their sales pitches and marketing collateral.

On the other side of the coin, if a consistent problem shows up on these cards (shipments are routinely arriving late or damage is most often reported from one carrier, for example), this would indicate a systemic problem that should be addressed by the supplier. Without any feedback though, management would be unaware the problem even exists. Maybe a customer might even write on the card, "Your order did not get here on time—we never have that problem with your competitors."

Well, that is information you need to act on. Why is it your competitors are able to deliver on time and you can not? Benchmarking key inventory and delivery processes can help you find out how they are making it happen. Then you can change your processes to meet that delivery timetable with greater reliability and consistency than competitors. Not doing so hurts your service reputation and possibly your sales down the line. But again, this information is usually not designed to be tabulated and correlated—and is only used to follow up on a specific delivery (and, most likely, to make the customer feel the supplier cares about the quality of service to them).

WARRANTY FORMS

As consumers, we are all used to buying products and filling out warranty cards or online warranty forms to register them with the manufacturer. The dirty little secret here is that you do not really need to fill out any forms in order to be eligible for the warranty—that warranty was included automatically with the purchase. You may have also noticed that you are asked on these forms seemingly irrelevant lifestyle questions, such as "Do you own a dog?" or "Do you play golf?" with the disclaimer that they are only asking these things because they want to know more about their customers.

Of course, if you have bought a refrigerator or a microwave or whatever, the maker really does not need to know whether you golf. However, the list broker the company sells your information to *does* want to know that, so he can, in turn, resell it to *GOLF* magazine or Titleist or Nike or whoever wants to market their golf products to consumers like you who play the game.

On the B2B side, however, many times meaningful marketing questions are not asked of customers at all on the warranty form. Take a look at the sample online one I have included in this chapter. You will see there is a comment box, and, if the customer even bothers to write something there, that is about all the supplier ever learns about the customer aside from the name, address and serial number of the product sold.

Once more—a missed opportunity. Let us say you have just sold a piece of production equipment. Whether you send them a written survey, have a customer rep call or send a salesperson in to follow up on the order, it is the perfect time to obtain some very valuable information from that customer. Questions such as:

- How are you going to use this equipment?
- What kind of volumes do you anticipate?
- What other types of equipment do you also purchase?
- How long do you expect this machine to last?
- What are the most frequent problems you have with these types of machines?
- Who is going to maintain it?

These kinds of queries allow the supplier to begin the process of expanding the relationship with the customer beyond that 1-time pur-

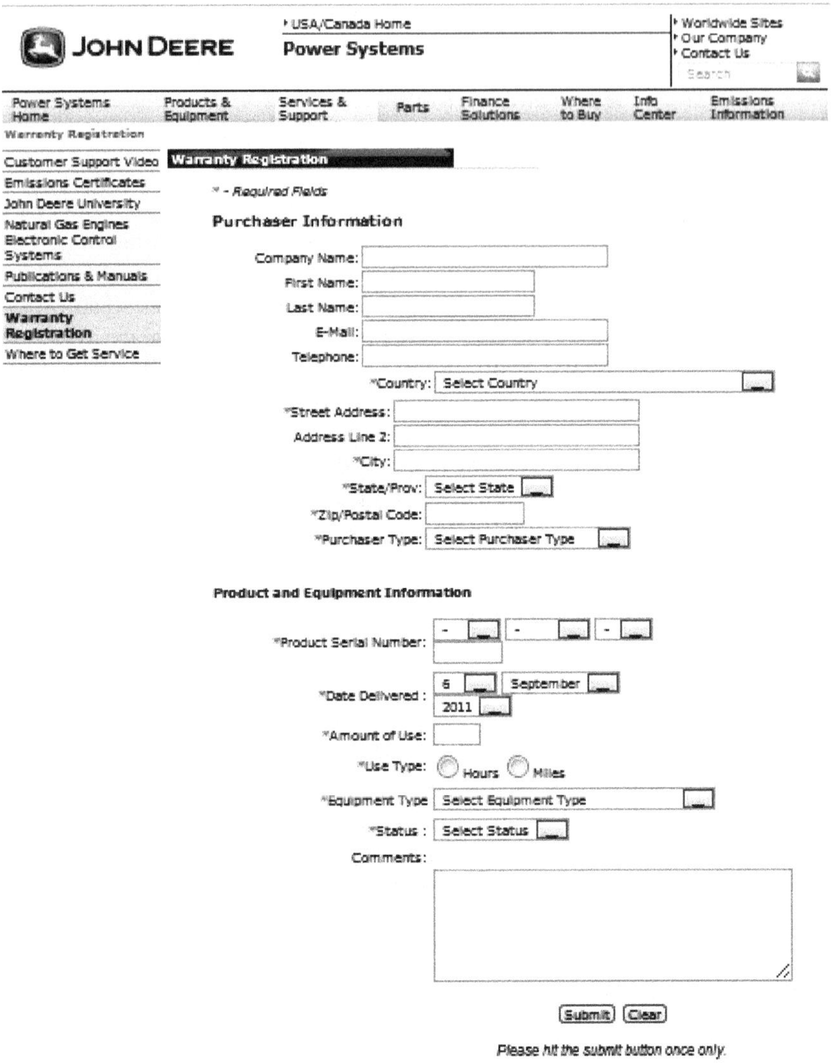

Figure 3.2.   Sample online warranty form.

chase. And quite frankly, the customer expects that to happen once they
have bought from a supplier. The warranty form is the perfect vehicle to
find out more about customers' needs—and, depending on what those
needs are, the suppliers can then follow up with offers to sell mainte-
nance, technical support, supplies and/or parts, and other pieces of
equipment. They can also be ready to help upgrade or replace the equip-

ment if they know approximately when a customer expects that to be necessary. And the supplier can learn more about how and why customers purchased their products so they can do a better job of communicating benefits to the next purchaser.

This all sounds like simple common sense marketing that any supplier should do; sell one thing to a customer and then figure out how to sell the next. But B2B companies all too often do not think that way. They simply complete the order and move on, waiting for the next opportunity to present itself.

CUSTOMER SERVICE

Customer service is what most companies consider their "inside sales" department, as opposed to the "outside" sales force that actually goes out and makes the calls on customers. While that sales force is out after new business, the customer service department is typically charged with maintaining the customer accounts already in place, on a day-to-day basis.

In our customer insight surveys, frequently customers will name one of their supplier's customer service representatives by name and cite that person as the main reason they do business with that supplier. That is because that person is an expert at building and maintaining a strong relationship with the customer—he knows what the customer ordered, knows the politics involved at both ends of the supply chain and will flag a potential problem coming down the road before trouble happens.

A good customer service rep also initiates corrective action as soon as he spots that problem—and finds ways to keep the supplier-customer relationship healthy in spite of it. The rep knows what to say and whom to call—and the customer comes to rely on the rep to address their ongoing needs with the supplier. This kind of personal relationship is always a powerful tool in company relationships that tend to gravitate toward the impersonal.

Now, again, imagine the wealth of information that suppliers' customer reps have about the customers they are assigned. Anyone who deals with a customer every day to the point where they can anticipate their needs has an amazing handle on how they work and who the power players are. But this information unfortunately remains in the rep's head in most cases. Nobody is asking the rep for that information or cataloguing or organizing it—so another very valuable source of customer insight is ignored.

CUSTOMER AUDITS

Customer audits in the B2B world are kind of a reverse customer insight survey. Instead of a supplier researching if a customer is happy with their service, a customer is prescreening the supplier to see if they will be able to meet their needs should the customer give them a substantial and, often, ongoing order.

That means the potential customer will visit the supplier's facilities to see if they have the capacity and the capability to satisfy the customer's requirements. This can be an extremely thorough and long-term process. If you recall the Glen Raven case study from Chapter 2, General Motors did an ongoing customer audit on GR that basically spanned 3 years.

Most customer audits are not that arduous, but they are crucial. For example, let us say a company is thinking about buying a truckload of a certain chemical every week from a supplier. That customer will want to know the right quality controls are in place, that they are going to get exactly the product they want every time, that the supplier's facility has the capacity to manufacture a truckload each week and that their personnel is well trained and know how to address safety issues.

Now, a customer audit, in the supplier's mind, is only about one question—"Did we pass so we can get the business?" But, even though this process is centered on the customer understanding the supplier's capabilities, there is also a really big opportunity here for the supplier to more fully understand what the customer wants—and to react accordingly to secure their business.

The customer is not stupid. They need to ensure that a supplier responsible for fulfilling a large ongoing order is going to be able to perform—and not put the business in jeopardy down the line. That is why the customer invests a lot of time, money and effort into developing a specific audit list. If the supplier can take that audit form, look over what the customer wants, understand why those things are important and how they can capitalize on them—well, that is simply Marketing 101.

But most suppliers do not take that extra step. Instead, if the customer wants to make sure the facility has a clean workplace at all times, the supplier has a kneejerk response and quickly straightens everything up at the facility before the visit. Just as in the sales call reports we discussed earlier in the chapter, the effort is not made to go beyond the simplistic facts—the "Who, What and Where" of the audit list. Instead, a genuine attempt should be made to answer the "Why" and the "How"—as in "Why is a clean workplace important to this customer?" and "How do we demonstrate our commitment to this particular requirement?"

Commitment is demonstrated by cleaning up all the yellow lines on the floor of the facility—making sure they are freshly painted and look clean and fresh; By putting into effect employee training and instituting and enforcing a policy that ensures everyone will clean up after themselves at all times; By stating in that policy that, when someone is in the middle of a repair project at the end of the day, they can not just leave

Vendor Audit Report

Details of Third Party Certifications
Details of previous audits by Site

PERSONS RESPONSIBLE FOR CONTACTS WITH SITE CONCERNING		
Department	Name	Number
Quality		
Technical		
Commercial		

DETAILED AUDIT REPORT (Add All Documentation Connected To The Audit)				
Document Type	Yes	No	Stored in a Central File	Sent as an Appendix To The Audit Report
Organisational Chart				
Certificate from the Authorities				
Third party certification				
Reports from previous Site audits				
List of products manufactured				
Production layout				
Process flow chart				
Supplier's booklet				
Audit questionnaire filled in				

VISIT TO THE FACILITIES	
Warehouse	
Manufacturing • Labelling system (raw materials, intermediates, finish products) • Computerised systems • Documentation (SOP, Batch Production Report.)	-
Quality Control, Quality Assurance and Laboratories - QA organisation - QC organisation - Certifications (detailed in general report) - Procedures - QA activities (release, customer complaints, change control, reprocess....) - Laboratories	
Training and Development	

All information contained within this document will be treated as confidential between the Supplier and Sydco.

File Location: Date Printed: Page 3 of 3

Figure 3.3. A simple customer audit form.

their tools laying around and the equipment in question open and exposed overnight.

In most cases, the supplier will learn valuable lessons from the customer. For example, in many cases it has been demonstrated that a clean workspace allows faster throughput, lower levels of inventory, faster change-over, and improved productivity. The supplier going through the motions of a clean work area misses the entire point.

Think about it—that customer has been purchasing the same products for years. They know all the good suppliers and they know what makes a supplier successful. They do not want a supplier to struggle—that will hurt them down the road. In essence, they are offering free process improvement consulting.

Suddenly, that spotless workplace becomes an overall mandate put in place by the supplier—a visible mandate easily recognized by the customer, whose comfort level is lifted far more than it would be by a hastily cleaned area designed to "get by" for the purposes of the audit. Successful customer insight is not just about knowing what a customer's requirements are—it is taking those requirements, dealing with why those requirements are important, and expanding on them to address the reasons *behind* those requirements.

I would like to share a few final thoughts on the different company processes I have just discussed. What they all have in common is the fact that they are all routine processes in which direct contact with the customer occurs, either through face-to-face, email, online, telephone or written modes of communication. Every time contact with customers happens is an opportunity to gain more insight into the supplier's relationships with them and how to strengthen and expand those relationships.

This is information that companies frequently pay consultants and third party companies such as PMG to dig out for them—*when it is already readily available to them internally*. While there are good reasons to hire outside researchers periodically, as we will discuss in the next section of this chapter, the fact is that, if a company creates continual and consistent systems to gather the info from the internal sources we have indicated and, just as importantly, share it with all relevant parties, those systems will aid your sales and management strategy immensely in expanding your market share with your current customers.

If those systems are not put in place, valuable information gets lost in the day-to-day shuffle and is never put to proper use. We estimate that over 90% of all companies just do not effectively exploit this kind of internal data. It is almost never done—and, when it is, it is certainly not done in any kind of systematic manner that would yield the results that it should.

So why *would not* a company do that? Seems like perfect common sense, does not it?

The main reason is that there is usually not a function in the company that is asking for this information. Instead, everyone's doing their specific jobs and not going beyond the immediate aims of those jobs. To be fair, no one asks them to, so it does not happen.

That is a shame—because the easiest way to expand your business is through those current customers. They are the "low-hanging fruit" that can feed your growth like nothing else. With current customers, the door is already open to your company—half the battle's won. You have already gone through the whole selling process with them—there is the second half of the battle. They know you and you know them and, hopefully, they are comfortable working with you. So why invest most development resources and personnel into trying to find new customers—when it is so much more efficient to just sell more to your existing customers?

Many suppliers stop trying to make that happen. They may have locked up 30% of the market and think they can not get any further with current customers. But think about it—you could double that share percentage and still have a lot of viable competition out there. There is no reason to stop trying to grow your share—and when you leverage customer contact through customer insight, you have created a multitude of future opportunities for your business.

THE CUSTOMER INSIGHT SURVEY

As I have said, a system for the internal cataloguing, exchange and interpretation of customer information should ideally be in place at a company. However, a customer insight survey, done on a regular basis, can be complimentary to this ongoing effort and complete the overall picture in a substantive way.

Customer insight, properly executed, has several distinct and powerful advantages over a company's own internal efforts and can act as a necessary reality check on those efforts. Those advantages include:

Objectivity

This is probably the biggest benefit an outside customer survey can offer. Bias can and does occur internally—each department has its own agenda and will frequently either consciously or unconsciously fit data to meet that agenda. It is just human nature. Salespeople, for example, can be reluctant to advance negative information that might threaten them or their jobs—like news that a competitor has increased their share with a customer. That kind of bias is easily overcome by an outside company, who will not have any "dog in the hunt" when doing their research and will stick to the facts they uncover.

Context

Another pitfall of internal information is that it can be highly anecdotal and specific in nature—and can possibly distort the big picture. An outside survey will find the proper context for its research findings so it can be viewed in the appropriate and most helpful way.

Accuracy

The survey methodology is designed to generate the most exact and precise findings. Instead of retrieving piecemeal bits of information over time, there is a concerted and concentrated effort to create a verified set of data that generates consistent and precise results.

Honesty

When a third party conducts interviews with your customers, those customers traditionally will open up more to a person who does not directly work for the supplier. They feel freer to criticize and to compliment a supplier's performance. The survey company acts as a buffer, allowing the customer to say things in a way they may feel uncomfortable saying face-to-face to the supplier. Think about when you went to high school—how many things did people say behind your back about you that you later heard about second-hand? Well, sad to say, many of us do not advance our social skills much beyond eleventh or twelfth grade—and we rarely will get an honest assessment of ourselves from someone we are directly talking to.

As you can see, all of these attributes that an independent customer insight project brings to the table are incredibly important. We will get more into the specifics of a customer insight survey in the next few chapters, but I would like to conclude this one with one more case study that illustrates why these types of surveys can be incredibly important in the B2B world—and how they are very different from consumer customer surveys.

CASE STUDY: PEERLESS MANUFACTURING CO.— "THE B2B CUSTOMER INSIGHT DIFFERENCE"

Warren Hayslip has been the chief operating officer at Peerless, whose main offices are located in Dallas, Texas, since 2009. Warren has worked with PMG at a number of the companies he is worked at over the years, because he is very familiar with our customer insight methodology with good reason—he was my original partner at PMG.

When he joined Peerless, he was determined to use the PMG methodology to understand just how Peerless stood with its customer base. I will let him describe the process and why it was important both to him personally and to the company from a strategic standpoint.

At Peerless, the survey work in the past was not as rigorous, not as comprehensive, and not as insightful as PMG's work. And I wanted to upgrade the market analysis of the company for a variety of reasons—I was relatively new to the company and I wanted to get a fresh unbiased look at the performance in terms of customers. If you are going to embark on major performance improvement programs, you want something more than loose anecdotal information—that information can be WRONG.

Two types of realms of data came from the initial customer insight survey. One was potentially rich quantitative competitive data, and the other was qualitative comments that added color and flavor. While the survey did not change the fundamental assumptions of the company, it gave empirical evidence on which decisions could be made.

We really focused on time to market and the importance of order lead times and delivery—that whole dimension of time performance. The survey helped us get a better grip on that dimension of our performance and the importance of that in the eyes of our customer. It was very important strategic information that gave us valuable insight into the marketplace. There was also a boatload of comments that we were able to track back to specific customers, so we knew where to focus on specific improvements.

Besides me as a newcomer wanting an accurate insight into the company, there was another reason I wanted the survey done by PMG—and that was for the rest of the organization. In many cases, people in the company already knew about our strengths and weaknesses, but it is what I call cloistered information—it does not get shared between departments and even specific personnel. That happens for a lot of reasons—people are busy and do not have time to communicate every little thing. And if you do not have an apparatus, you have incomplete inside communication.

The customer insight survey provides a common base of information from which multiple parties can gain insights, particularly, in this case, the customer support side. Customers have different situations and their needs vary. Understanding specific segments and customers allows you to become more actionable in your strategy.

We had group meetings to share the survey information. All of management was involved; there were multiple meetings and four presentations at different offices. We shared it overseas, and we shared it with the board of directors. As a matter of fact, when I brought on a new head of quality assurance, I gave him the survey and said, "This is one of the first things you need to study." What's really important is that you can't just stick this data in a book and put it away on a shelf somewhere, you have to take it and use it to improve performance.

PMG has a methodology strictly tailored to the B2B reality. That makes their survey a product that is much more valuable to a B2B company. This stuff works—I have 14 years of experience on the corporate side that proves it does.

—Warren Hayslip
Chief Operating Officer
Peerless

Thank you, Warren. In our next chapter, we will begin to drill deeper into the customer insight survey mechanics, so you can gain a better understanding of the critical questions it asks and why the answers can be incredibly valuable to any supplier.

CHAPTER 4

CRITICAL QUESTIONS

Customer insight made it clear where we had to focus. That had serious true marketing value. I had never seen it before and I have not seen it since.

—John Schneiter
Founder and Former CEO
Global Spec

GLOBAL SPEC CASE STUDY: ASKING THE CRITICAL QUESTIONS

Engineer John Schneiter was completely frustrated by an ongoing problem he had in his position at General Electric: finding the right parts to order for projects his department was building. In those preinternet days, the only way to hunt for those parts was to obtain engineering catalogues and search through them one at a time. From what he could see, around 20% of an active engineer's valuable time was being wasted—not just by having to search for these parts in a catalogue, but also just trying to hunt down the right catalogue in the first place!

In 1995, on a clear blue sky September day, however, John had an epiphany. He was using the brand new Mosaic web browser to search on the internet and was struck by a thought: What if all those catalogues from different suppliers could be compiled in one place—creating one master online catalogue that was instantly searchable? While you could not charge engineers to use that kind of service, as they had never paid a dime to find a part in their lives, you *could* charge the suppliers directly

B2B Customer Insight: The Proven Path to Growth, pp. 45–59
Copyright © 2012 by Information Age Publishing
All rights of reproduction in any form reserved.

for the privilege of being included in this breakthrough one-stop internet shop.

By October 1995, John and three other partners were so excited about this idea that they put a name on it—GlobalSpec—and set up an initial barebones website to begin developing the concept further. By early 1996, they got their first suppliers to commit to being a part of it. Finally, a couple of years later, John left GE to work on this new venture full-time. Because this was the first time John had started a company from scratch, coupled with the fact that internet marketing was still also a very new concept, he still felt he needed some outside guidance on how to properly develop this endeavor.

To gain more perspective, he joined up with a think tank of manufacturer CEOs who were exchanging information in order to help each other's businesses. One of those gatherings was at a company where we happened to be doing one of our customer insight presentations. I will let John Schneiter tell the story from there.

> We were invited to attend a report by the marketing organization, Priority Metrics Group, Inc., where I met John. I was absolutely blown away. He seemed to be doing something I had not seen anyone else do—providing an effective blend of quantitative and qualitative data.
>
> At the time, GlobalSpec had gone from 15 people to 115 people in about 6 months. We were struggling with growth and the insanity of adding that many people and functions at once. Marketing was not being handled well and we were desperately looking for something that would help us do the right things. I thought maybe a guy like John could apply what he did to both sides of what we did—the supplier and the user sides. That way, we could understand if we were doing the right thing and we could also give both sides what they needed.
>
> John delivered. He not only helped us guide our marketing efforts, but the site design efforts as well. Most importantly, he helped us to prioritize where we put our time and resources. The customer insight projects he did for GlobalSpec in those early days shaped our business, as we translated that insight into strategic action.
>
> John told us where the danger zones were and where the opportunities were, so we knew what to do in order to appeal to the user side, as well as create value on the supplier side. By providing us with a list of value attributes, as well as indicating which of those attributes were the most important, we had the ability to sit in a room and map out future action. We could also see where we were doing well against the competition and where we were doing poorly, as well as what the suppliers and users cared about and what they did not. A couple of the charts that John generated for us are part of GlobalSpec's institutional knowledge that are still used today.
>
> We even realized some side benefits we had not anticipated. For example, John and his folks talked to quite a number of people on the user side.

He provided us with names that indicated they would be happy to be part of a user community group and give us feedback on directions we were considering. In other words, John helped us create an ongoing no-cost focus group that we could use on a regular basis.

There were a lot of hurricane-like winds going on while we were building GlobalSpec. The tech bubble was bursting in 2000 and people suddenly thought the internet was a fad. Our existing customers, however, understood what we were doing and the value, thanks to the direction we were given by PMG's customer insight—and that is why we made it through the dark days.

—John Schneiter
GlobalSpec

GlobalSpec was a unique opportunity for us, because we could help define their business from the get-go, rather than jump in after they were further down the line and more established. It was also good timing on their part. As John noted, internet start-ups suddenly fell out of favor without much warning in 2000—but because GlobalSpec implemented our information correctly, the company survived and went on to prosper, while other dot coms, with their feet not so firmly planted on the ground, fell by the wayside.

What we were able to do for Global Spec was answer their *three critical questions* through customer insight:

- Performance: How well are they performing compared to customer expectations?
- Importance: What attributes are most important to their customers?
- Competition: What is their competitive position in the marketplace?

At PMG, we have identified these three questions as the most crucial ones for companies to ask about their customers. They are the questions that come up again and again—and the answers consistently provide clear strategic direction. I would like to review what those three key questions are all about, and then discuss the importance of how they all relate to each other.

CRITICAL QUESTION #1: PERFORMANCE

Figure 4.1 details some of typical performance attributes we measured through customer insight for one of our clients:

As you can see, there were 30-odd performance attributes that our client felt were important to look at in this particular case. This list was generated from conversations we had with the sales force, customer service reps and quality improvement teams, reviewing call reports and warranty

Performance Attributes

Product Performance
1. Colorfastness
2. Consistency of Quality
3. Dimensional Stability
4. Durability
5. Ease of Fabrication
6. General Appearance
7. Performance in Your Application
8. Strength
9. Water Repellency

Product Development/Design
10. Breadth and Variety of Product Line
11. Capability to Develop Creative Solutions
12. Quality of Color, Style, and Design

Deliveries & Shipments
13. Accuracy of Shipments
14. Minimum Order Size
15. On-Time Deliveries
16. Order Lead-Times
17. Packaging & Labeling

Sales & Customer Support:
18. Complaint Handling
19. Customer Service
20. Ease of Placing an Order
21. Product and Industry Knowledge
22. Sales Representation
23. Timeliness of Response to Inquiries
24. Warranty Claim Handling

Technical Support
25. Ability to Solve Technical Problems
26. Courtesy/Professionalism of Technical Staff
27. Efficient Resolution of Technical Issues
28. Responsiveness to Your Requests

Price and Value
29. Competitive Price
30. Overall Value

Overall Satisfaction
31. Overall Satisfaction

Priority Metrics Group

Acme

Figure 4.1.   Performance attributes for a typical customer insight survey.

claims, and other sources. How these attributes are worded and described will vary, depending on what industry the business operates in and the nature of their business. It is important, therefore, to work within the specific attributes of each industry, as well as using the specifications that are unique to each company's products and services, to give the best and clearest possible perspective on them. In other words, we always want to "talk the language" of whatever business we work with so that everyone is on the same page and misunderstandings are rare.

Once we have identified the key performance attributes that are worth measuring, we find out how their customers rate them on each individual attribute, as in Figure 4.2.

Obviously, how the customer "grades" the supplier on these individual attributes is imperative to look at. The surprising fact is, however, these ratings are almost meaningless to the supplier in question—until the second customer insight critical question is answered.

CRITICAL QUESTION #2: IMPORTANCE

Measuring performance attributes without measuring the individual importance of each of those attributes can result in some very misguided

Company Performance > Average Ratings

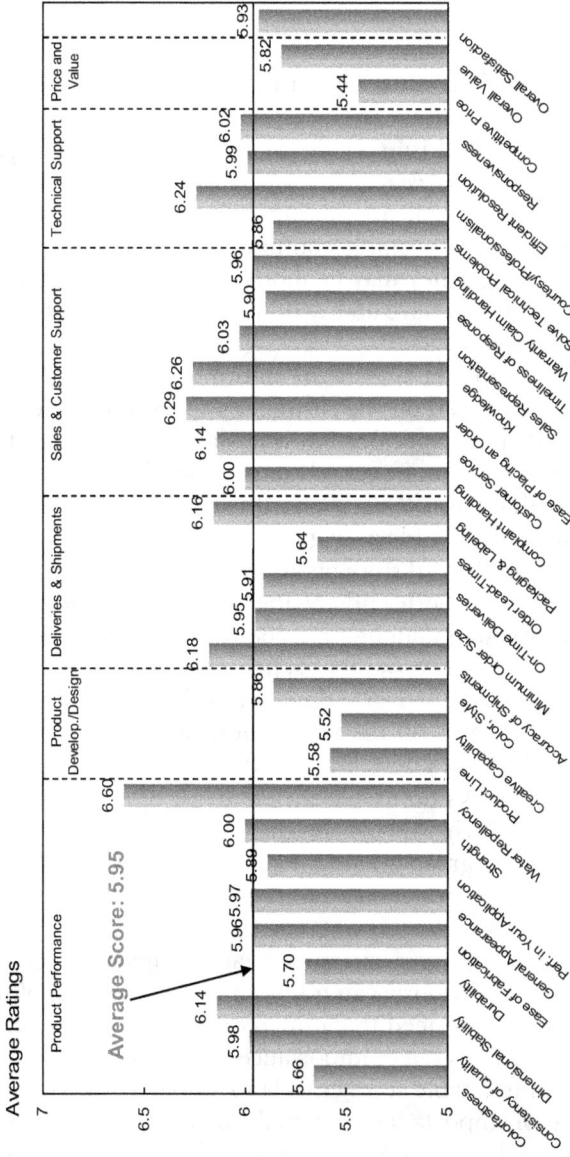

Average Ratings

Average Score: 5.95

Product Performance

Dimensional Stability
Consistency of Quality 5.66
Durability 5.98
Ease of Fabrication 6.14
General Appearance 5.70
Perf. in Your Application 5.96 5.97
Strength 5.89
Water Repellency 6.00
Product Line 6.60

Product Develop./Design

Creative Capability 5.58 5.52
Color Style 5.86
Accuracy of Shipments 6.18

Deliveries & Shipments

Minimum Order Size 5.95 5.91
On-Time Deliveries 5.64
Order Lead-Times 6.16
Packaging & Labeling 6.00

Sales & Customer Support

Complaint Handling 6.14
Customer Service 6.29 6.26
Ease of Placing an Order 6.03
Knowledge 5.90 5.96
Sales Representation
Timeliness of Response
Warranty Claim Handling 6.86
Solve Technical Problems

Technical Support

Courtesy/Professionalism 6.24
Efficient Resolution 5.99 6.02
Responsiveness
Competitive Price 5.82

Price and Value

Overall Value 5.44
Overall Satisfaction 5.93

Priority Metrics Group

Acme

Figure 4.2. Average ratings.

49

moves. Unfortunately, a lot of companies stop at simply understanding how well they are performing in the customers' eyes; we have found this is woefully insufficient. It prompts a company to overreact to areas of strength as well as weakness. If a customer praises a performance attribute, the supplier thinks it needs to keep promoting its capability in that area. If a customer complains about another attribute, the supplier thinks every expense and effort must be put into fixing that negative situation immediately.

It all comes down to this; *if you do not know how important a performance attribute is to your customers, you have no idea what is worth reacting to and what is not.* In other words, you are setting policy in the dark. Even more importantly, you might be simply continuing to do certain things in certain ways, even though they may be more costly or time consuming, simply because it is how you have always done those things and you *think* it is what your customer expects.

For example, a supplier may be monitoring their manufacturing processes for a product based on the customer's specs, without ever knowing whether each individual specification is actually important to the performance of the product. I am frequently amazed to discover just how often a spec is asked for that has *nothing* to do with actual product performance—and that the customer would easily give up if questioned about it.

It brings to mind the old story about the mother preparing a roast for the oven—she cuts off both ends of the roast before she puts it in the roasting pan. Her young daughter asks her why she always does that—the mother replies, "I do not know, that is how your grandmother always did it." The girl then goes to her grandmother and asks the same question—why did she cut the ends off the roast before she cooked it? The grandmother says she does not know either ... that is the way *her* mother did it.

Finally, the girl tracks down her ancient great grandmother to try and get the real answer: "Why did you cut the ends of the roast before you put it in the oven?" The great grandma smiles and answers, "I only had a small pan. It is the only way I could fit the roast in it."

When you have 30-odd (or, in some cases, even more) performance attributes involved with your customer relationships, you need a basis to prioritize them. You obviously can not put the same level of effort into all of them and you do not need to. Some require more and some require a lot less—because the degree of importance to the customer can vary from absolutely critical to a table stake criteria to a nonfactor. Without measuring that degree of importance, you could be aggressively promoting an attribute that frankly means nothing to your buyer! True customer satisfaction comes from fulfilling their most important needs as completely as possible—and allocating resources to those performance attributes most critical to them.

For example, another one of our clients, Bob Barker Company, delivers supplies for use by inmates of correctional facilities. When they were in the early years of their business, they routinely heard that these facilities needed to always have these kinds of supplies on hand—they simply could not afford to run out of them. Bob Barker, the Company's founder and namesake, decided then and there that he would make one of his main selling points the fact that his company would ship an order out the same day if it was called in by a certain time. This seemed like an obvious solution to a customer problem and, from the very start, Bob Barker made every effort to be customer driven.

The reality, however, was that, because of security and bureaucracy issues, the shipments spent a great deal of time being checked in and inventoried when they were delivered to a facility. That meant it might take up to a week before the supplies made their way to any of the inmates. Same day delivery was just not important to these facilities, it was all about refilling their inventory to avoid problems down the line resulting from a needed product being out of stock. Yet, this extra emphasis on quick shipping was costing Bob Barker a lot of extra time, effort and money.

After our customer insight survey revealed otherwise, they were able to selectively offer next day service without causing any disruptions for their customers. Of course, this same customer insight survey also showed that these customers ranked Bob Barker very high on speed of delivery—but that performance attribute ended up ranking very low in importance. Without complete and correct information, management's desire to respond to the "voice of the customer" can result in added procedures and unnecessary expenditures.

Figure 4.3 shows our measurements of how important each attribute is to a supplier's circle of customers.

It is interesting to compare this chart with the performance rating chart featured earlier in this chapter, but let me point out one thing in particular. One of the highest rated performance attributes in that earlier chart was "water repellency." All of the customers thought that the supplier did an excellent job delivering a product with this performance attribute.

Good news for the supplier, right? If that is all the company had to work with, it would be wildly enthusiastic over those sky-high marks and sell that performance attribute as hard as possible. However, if they have access to the derived importance chart above as well, that enthusiasm would soon be dampened in spite of the high water repellency. That is because that particular attribute is actually ranked the *lowest* in importance by their customers. It is the same story as Bob Barker's next day delivery—the supplier is really good at doing something … *that customers*

Company Performance > Derived Importance

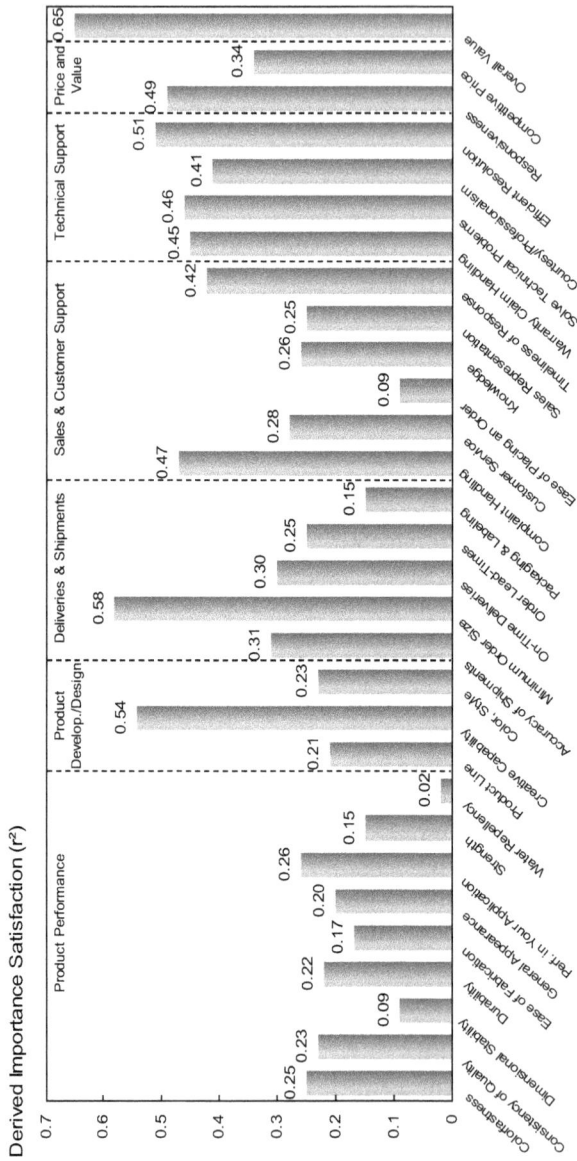

Derived Importance Satisfaction (r²)

Figure 4.3.   Attribute importance.

put little emphasis on! And to be fair to both companies, you can not really know that until you have had a proper customer insight survey done.

There is a subtle distinction that may be made here. Just because an attribute is evaluated as being low in importance does not necessarily mean it is of no importance to the customer. Often, it suggests that the attribute has become an expected element of the overall product and service mix—a table stake if you will. Differentiating between a table stake and an unimportant attribute requires a broader understanding of the business environment and the supplier-customer relationship that comes through qualitative questions in the survey and further analysis.

In this case, with both charts in hand, some serious soul searching at this company may be in order. If water repellency actually costs them significant production costs to add to the product, why bother to continue trying to improve that performance attribute? If the customer does not care about this feature as much as other attributes, or if it has become a table stake—why should the manufacturer give more of it? Redirecting resources to other attributes would allow them to improve the value that customers receive and result in a stronger and more defensible competitive position.

As important as the two critical questions of performance and importance are, there is still one more question that needs to be answered to really put everything in the proper perspective for complete customer insight. Once we add competitive position to the survey question, we can gain a full strategic way of thinking about any company's future direction.

CRITICAL QUESTION #3: COMPETITIVE POSITION

Assessing competitive position is one area where B2B can be strikingly similar to B2C. Our consumer, buying toothpaste in the aisle at the grocery store, will be assessing relative worth of each product and making trade-offs as he chooses between the various competitive offerings. For example, does he want whitening or does he want a "fresh breath" mouthwash component? Does he want a stand-up dispenser or the traditional tube? The name brand or the cheaper store brand?

The B2B customer does essentially the same thing on an ongoing basis. That B2B customer does differ in some respects from an individual consumer—as shown in the table in the Introduction to this book. For example, she may be part of a buying group and she probably knows significantly more about the product than an end user—maybe even as much as the producer. The B2B customer uses this information in a systematic and logical way to make a purchase decision and determine the share of their total spend that will go to a given supplier. But, even if a supplier is currently the sole source for a product they are buying, they grew to that position by demonstrating a competitive advantage over similar suppliers. If I am that supplier and want to continue to be that sole source, I need to make sure I maintain that competitive advantage—because my customer is constantly going to be asking, "Am I getting the most I can from my supplier?"

Obviously, competitive position, then, certainly belongs as one of the three critical questions we must answer about any supplier's relationship with its customers. But not everybody agrees—an executive familiar with our methodology once joined a company that used an internationally respected research firm to do their customer insight research. He was shocked to learn that *they did not measure competitive position at all*. Which, ironically, gave *us* a better competitive position in the eyes of that client— enabling us to up replace the better known research firm.

When we measure competitive position, we measure how key performance attributes fare against the competition. You can see from the chart above how we typically map this out—the supplier can very clearly see at a glance where it is falling behind other competing companies (attributes in red) and where it outshines them (attributes in blue).

Still, this leaves out the other critical question of importance. If we return to the water repellency example, you can see from the chart that our supplier scores ahead of the competition in this attribute. But again, the customer does not care that much about it—so it does not matter as much that the supplier excels in this area.

The truth is the measurements from all three critical questions must be taken into account to create a final visual tool that can show where a company must excel—and other areas that are table stakes or have a lower priority for improvement.

THE COMPANY PERFORMANCE IMPROVEMENT MAP

How Performance and Importance Are Both Required for True Customer Insight

What you are looking at in Figure 4.5 is frequently the most valuable tool we can provide to a client. This *Company Performance Improvement Map* breaks down our measurements into an easy to access visual diagram through which our client's management can begin their strategic planning for the future.

Let us go through this chart one quadrant at a time, because each has a distinct interpretation that helps clarify how you view the attributes it contains. For example, the lower left quadrant contains what we call *"Long*

Company Performance > Net Scores

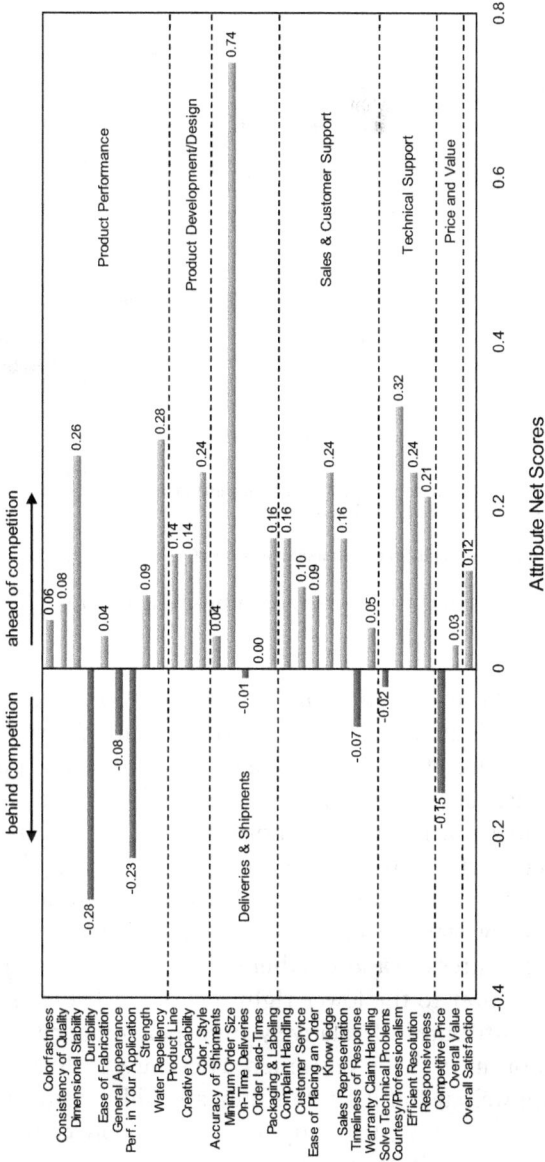

Figure 4.4. Competitive position.

Customer Satisfaction

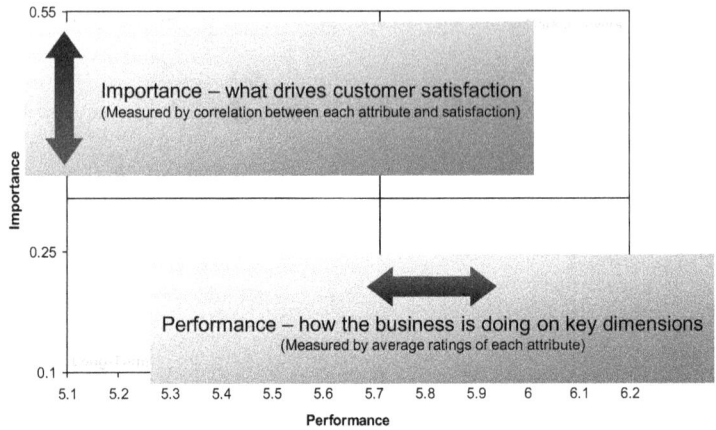

0.55

Importance – what drives customer satisfaction
(Measured by correlation between each attribute and satisfaction)

Importance

0.25

Performance – how the business is doing on key dimensions
(Measured by average ratings of each attribute)

0.1

| 5.1 | 5.2 | 5.3 | 5.4 | 5.5 | 5.6 | 5.7 | 5.8 | 5.9 | 6 | 6.1 | 6.2 |

Performance

Two key elements of satisfaction are performance and importance. Understanding satisfaction requires a knowledge of both dimensions.

Conclusion: Performance is an insufficient measure of customer satisfaction

Figure 4.5.   Construction of the performance improvement map.

Term Opportunities," those attributes that are of low importance, and where the customer has evaluated the company to be relatively weak in their performance. These are attributes that the client did not score particularly well on, but also, at the same time, are not really of great concern to customers. That does not mean you ignore them. The fact that the customer is voicing concern is a reality. But improving these attributes is not something that needs to be done urgently; because the importance just is not there, you do not want to have to make significant investments of money and other resources to address them.

Now, let us move over to the lower right quadrant. These are what we call *"Table Stakes,"* attributes of relatively high performance, but still of relatively low importance to the customer. These are performance areas that you are doing well at fulfilling, but they are still not all that important to the supplier. However, the supplier has probably come to expect you to do well at them, so it is a mistake to back off on them (unless it is a specific service, like Bob Barker's same day delivery service, that the customer absolutely does not need and will not be concerned to see it go).

Attributes in this area of the Improvement Map usually suggest the minimal levels of quality that the buyer expects from all suppliers—the "table stakes" that everyone has to bring to get in the game. Chances are all of your competition routinely provides many of these performance attributes just as you do, so doing them well will not make you stand out from the pack. They will just qualify you to be *in* the pack, as they demonstrate you are a viable supplier.

Let us continue on to the upper left quadrant, tagged as *"Improvement Priorities"* attributes of low performance, but that are also of relatively high importance. Clearly, this is where a supplier is most vulnerable. If your performance in one area is relatively low (at a level that the customer considers to be below their standards of performance), and that same area is very important, this is a situation that needs to be addressed as soon as possible. These are the kinds of crucial factors that could cost you a customer down the line.

If that is our bad news quadrant, the upper right quadrant is definitely our good news one. Attributes here are what we call *"Market Levers,"* having high performance and high importance. This is where you will find the attributes that differentiate you in the marketplace and provide the most powerful sales points for a supplier's marketing. When you send salespeople out into the field, these are the attributes you want them to talk about.

Now, often those salespeople will come back and tell you it is all about hitting the lowest price. In truth and with evidence to back you up, you can say, "Our prices may be a little higher, but this is what you are getting for that extra money." As we discussed in Chapter 2, this is where *value* comes into play—and your Market Levers are your living embodiment of that value.

This Performance Improvement Map lays it out for everyone at a company. It lets everyone know, from top to bottom, from hourly worker to CEO, from accounting to operations, where the focus needs to be and what the priorities are that make a difference in the marketplace. Rather than listen to random bits of anecdotal information from salespeople anxious to close a sale the easiest way possible (virtually always by lowering the price), management now has a unified vision on what needs to be improved internally (upper left quadrant) and what value should be reinforced to the customer (upper right quadrant). Clear marching orders can be given and a unified direction can be set, eliminating the all too familiar scenario of five different departments trying to force five different visions into the company mix.

Ideally, what should eventually happen is what we refer to as "resource alignment"—attributes that are the least important to your customers will be the ones in which you show your weakest performance, and your stron-

Company Performance > Improvement Map

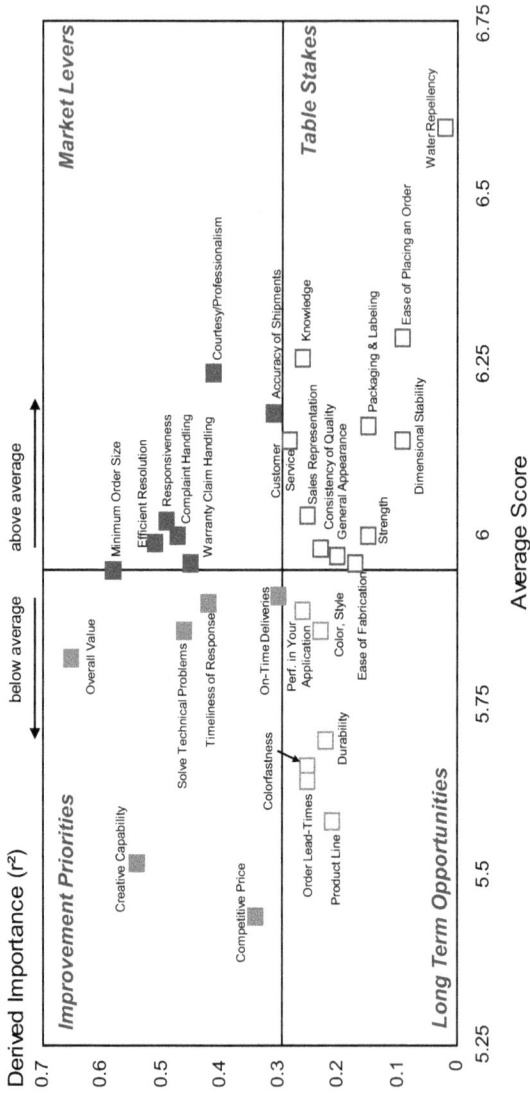

Figure 4.6. Performance improvement map.

gest performance is in those attributes that are the most important to your customers. That may never be perfectly realized, but it is what a company should work toward.

CONTEC CASE STUDY: LEVERAGING THE DATA

I would like to conclude this chapter by sharing how one client, Contec, Inc., used exactly this kind of survey data aggressively to grow their business. I will let the Contec CEO, Jack McBride, relate the story:

> In our largest market, we sell primarily through two large distributors, but we had to work hard to make our way into those companies. A competitor had been their primary supplier for 20 years and we wanted to take that business away. Using PMG's survey, we went back to that distributor and showed them, in black and white, how we stacked up against the competing company they used. They could see Contec was better in almost every category. They clearly understood the message—and, since their people are out in the field every day, they knew that the data were right. We said, "You should switch to us!"—and they did. That rolled half a million dollars worth of business our way.
>
> —Jack McBride
> Chief Executive Officer
> Contec

So how exactly do we prepare and distribute our survey questionnaires —so that we are able to ensure the most accurate data when it comes to answering the three critical questions we have discussed here? In the next chapter, we will delve into the PMG survey methodology and reveal a few of the innovative systems we have developed over the years.

CHAPTER 5

CUSTOMER INSIGHT METHODOLOGY

Sound management decisions are based on good customer feedback. Without understanding what the customer values, it is hard to make good business decisions.

—John Mixson
Director of Marketing
National Gypsum

NATIONAL GYPSUM CASE STUDY: THE RIGHT DATA MAKES THE RIGHT DIFFERENCE

When the "Great Recession" hit in 2008, the industries immediately hit the hardest were those associated with housing. One of our clients, National Gypsum Company, one of the largest gypsum board manufacturers in the world and a huge provider of drywall products, was certainly not exempt from the downturn.

Now, when an economic calamity of this scope hits, costs associated with conducting consumer research can be one of the first categories to be eliminated from a company's marketing budget. We had been providing National Gypsum with customer insight surveys since 1997, and we were pleased to see that National not only realized how important this data was, but has continued to ask for customer research from PMG during the last few difficult years.

B2B Customer Insight: The Proven Path to Growth, pp. 61–76
Copyright © 2012 by Information Age Publishing
All rights of reproduction in any form reserved.

John Mixson, National Gypsum's Director of Marketing, explains the value the company derives from doing regular survey work with us:

> Since 1997 we have conducted the same survey every 3 years. The first survey was designed to answer certain specific questions regarding our direct customers—questions such as, "What do you really value the most?" "How is National Gypsum doing relative to what you value?" "How are we doing in relation to our competition?"
>
> Our main goal with the surveys is to have a recurring process and keep our finger on the pulse of what our customers care about. From those surveys, we would shape initiatives based on the data and take action to correct things or make things better.
>
> For example, we made product quality issues a focal point. We did a study with drywall contractors around specific product working properties. Based on our findings, we made specific changes. As an example, we took a hard look at the edge consistency of our drywall. When you handle that drywall, you want the edges to be durable, but still take a nail or screw effectively when the product is installed. Our plants have the ability to adjust the product's edge profile, and we want to ensure our edges match the market's specific requirements.
>
> The next survey showed improvement in this area and we tracked toward the higher end of this particular attribute ranking, which was right where we wanted to be.
>
> PMG has a great ability to digest large sets of complex data and distill it down to "This is what the data really says, here's what really matters, and this is the math behind it." You have to know what you can conclude based on the data and where you have to be careful not to overreach, based on the statistical relevance.
>
> Doing these surveys over time helps to identify trends and makes sure you understand the competitive landscape. And it helps you to be consistent. In tough economic times, simply being consistent makes you a leader.
>
> —John Mixson
> Director of Marketing
> National Gypsum

National Gypsum's views its product quality and customer service as a competitive advantage. Implementing and prioritizing action initiatives based on our customer insight helps give National an important edge over other suppliers—an edge that it continues to build on and maintain.

As John made clear in the above case study, our customer insight surveys are respected because of their solid statistical methodology. In this chapter, we are going to talk about that methodology as well as how we design and execute the survey questionnaires to provide the most comprehensive and credible data, as well as the highest possible response rates. As we do so, we will walk you through a sample questionnaire, so you can see for yourself just how our customer insight surveys work.

APPROACHING OUR CLIENT'S CUSTOMERS

When we prepare to go out to our clients' customers with a customer insight survey, we always keep this one principle in mind: *anything related to the survey is a professional communication and should be treated with no less respect and care than any other important business interaction.*

If our clients were sending their customers a notice of a price increase, for example, they would certainly want to make sure that letter had the exact right language and that nobody's name was misspelled. While a survey doesn't contain that kind of bad news (fortunately), it still adds up to a little bit of inconvenience for the person we're asking to fill it out; it stands to reason, then, that we want to do it as politely and professionally as possible.

That means no cold calling and no dropping a survey in the mail without first paving the way. It's important to note that PMG is representing our clients in this process; we don't want to make our clients look bad to their customers by approaching the survey in anything less than a professional manner. We also want to drive home the message about why the supplier is coming to them with this survey; it's to say that they care about them to such an extent that they're soliciting their input to improve their business relationship, as well as the quality of product and service they provide.

You also have to keep in mind that the survey questionnaire generally needs to be completed, or at least partially done, by a senior executive at a company. These men and women are in positions of high level leadership and expect to be treated a certain way. They're also usually very pressed for time and completing surveys isn't an activity that's at the top of their to-do lists; that means we have to have a process in place that introduces the survey in such a way that makes them as comfortable as possible with the concept and the actual task.

That requires us to create any survey documentation, correspondence and material with great concern and care. To that end, we first spend a great deal of time double checking a forthcoming survey's recipients' list, making sure names are spelled correctly (to the point where we make sure a first name is spelled "John" and not "Jon") and that addresses are exactly right.

Next, we send out a letter on our client's company letterhead to each of their customers announcing the survey. That letter talks about the fact that the supplier is doing this survey because it values the customer's opinion and wants to improve. It goes on to say that the supplier has hired PMG and that we will be contacting the customer in question shortly with the actual survey materials.

This introductory letter is designed to do two things. First of all, since the customer may not know anything at all about PMG, the letter validates us; when we finally do contact them, they'll know who we are and why we are contacting them. Even though we may have been the ones to physically send out the letter, it appears as though the supplier has actually begun the process. That allows us to simply slide in and take over after this "official" introduction.

Second of all, the letter heightens the importance of the survey process; it "announces" the survey is coming in a way designed to demonstrate that it's significant. The survey doesn't just fly in the door without any warning to the customers; this separate letter indicates that this is an important business matter that deserves to be seriously considered and completed.

THE SURVEY QUESTIONNAIRE DESIGN

Shortly after the introductory letter is sent to all the desired customers for the survey, we follow up by mailing a hard copy of the actual survey questionnaire, along with a stamped self-addressed envelope in which they can return the survey after it's been completed. (By the way, we even go the extra step of placing the correct amount and nationality of postage on each return envelope for international customers.)

Since this isn't a mass mailing but, rather, one targeted to a strictly B2B population, the survey itself needs to be designed more like a business correspondence; we definitely don't want to come off like we're talking down to the executives as if we're administering the SAT to a student. Obviously, you can't tell a company CEO he has to use a #2 pencil or completely fill in the bubbles for multiple choice questions. Again, you must approach these executives respectfully, not condescendingly, and avoid making the survey sound in any way like an onerous chore.

We also need to make the survey questionnaire as easy and foolproof as possible. That's why we put together the survey (which is typically four pages long) in a booklet or tabloid format. That way, there are no pages to be lost, no staples can come out, it's all of one piece and the executive can see instantly what's entailed. Our survey format is not some kind of industry standard, but we've found it just absolutely works the best for our purposes in this kind of arena.

The front of the survey booklet will contain a cover letter and instructions, so the customers are reminded of what it's all about and why our client would like them to fill it out. Most importantly, it will have a PMG name and the project manager's direct phone number at the bottom of the page, in case the executive needs to contact us directly with a question about the survey. We want to enable easy access so they can reach us quickly.

A typical questionnaire front page is reproduced below:

2011 ABC CUSTOMER SURVEY

I. Survey Sponsor

ABC Company
1234 W. 76th Street
Anywhere, SC 12548

II. Instructions for the Respondent:

This survey has been designed to **critically evaluate the performance of ABC Company as a supplier of widgets.**
The basic approach of this survey is to ask you—the respondent—for your **honest, objective perceptions of how well ABC and your best alternate supplier are performing versus your expectations**. By "best alternate supplier" we mean that one alternate supplier which can best supply you with products that you could substitute for those you currently purchase from ABC Company. Please rate only a single "best alternate supplier" throughout the entire survey. If you do not have such an alternate supplier, please rate ABC Company alone.
Behind this cover, you will find a questionnaire covering a variety of performance attributes. To complete this survey, you will need as little as 10-15 minutes. However, we do encourage you to use as much time as you need to thoughtfully consider your responses to the questions—as they will be taken seriously. After you have completed the survey, please mail the questionnaire back to us in the enclosed self- addressed envelope.

III. Correspondence:

If you have questions or care to discuss any aspect of this survey, please contact:

Priority Metrics Group, Inc.
Customer Survey Division
PO Box 1943
Spartanburg, SC 29304
Telephone: (800) 742-0461
Project Manager: John Barrett
jbarrett@pmgco.com

Thank You.

As you can tell, that cover letter/instruction sheet tells the recipient everything he or she needs to know about the survey contents; who's it for, who's doing it, who they can contact with questions, how long it will take and so forth. It's very straight forward and fact-based, and intentionally so.

When they next open the survey booklet, they'll be able to see the main contents of the survey questionnaire and what they are being asked to do. We created it this way so it feels very out in the open and not secretive at all. As a matter of fact, one of the reasons we shy away from doing these surveys on the web (even though we do offer that service) is that when you answer a question on a web page and click through to the next one, you have no idea how many more of those web pages you'll need to deal with. Is it 3 more pages? Is it 50? If you've ever done an online questionnaire, you know how frustrating it can be to not know how long it will tie you up. Our simple three page questionnaire layout (the survey concludes on the fourth back page of the booklet) eliminates that problem.

On the next two pages, you will see the sample contents of those three survey questionnaire pages that we have prepared especially for this book:

2011 ABC COMPANY CUSTOMER SURVEY

Please rate the performance of ABC Company and your best alternate supplier. To do so, circle the appropriate numerical score for each performance attribute listed on the scales below. If you feel you are not qualified to rate any question, circle "NA" (not applicable) and skip on to the next appropriate question. In this survey, 1 represents the *worst* possible score and 7 represents the *best*, as depicted below:

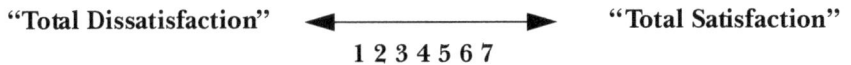

"Total Dissatisfaction" ◄─────────► **"Total Satisfaction"**
1 2 3 4 5 6 7

1. Product Performance/Quality:	ABC Company	Best Alternate Supplier
1a) Consistent Quality	1 2 3 4 5 6 7	1 2 3 4 5 6 7
1b) Performance on Your Equipment	1 2 3 4 5 6 7	1 2 3 4 5 6 7

Please add comments or suggestions for product performance and quality improvement:

_____
_____
_____

2. **Delivery & Customer Service:**

	ABC Company	Best Alternate Supplier
2a) Order Lead-Times	1 2 3 4 5 6 7	1 2 3 4 5 6 7 NA
2b) Sample Lead-Times	1 2 3 4 5 6 7	1 2 3 4 5 6 7 NA
2c) On-Time Delivery	1 2 3 4 5 6 7	1 2 3 4 5 6 7 NA
2d) Responsiveness to Inquiries	1 2 3 4 5 6 7	1 2 3 4 5 6 7 NA
2e) Overall Service Quality	1 2 3 4 5 6 7	1 2 3 4 5 6 7 NA

Please add comments or suggestions for delivery and customer service improvement:

_____

_____

_____

3. **Sales Support:**

3a) Industry Knowledge	1 2 3 4 5 6 7	1 2 3 4 5 6 7 NA
3b) Product Knowledge	1 2 3 4 5 6 7	1 2 3 4 5 6 7 NA
3c) Contact Frequency	1 2 3 4 5 6 7	1 2 3 4 5 6 7 NA
3d) Timely Response to Inquiries	1 2 3 4 5 6 7	1 2 3 4 5 6 7 NA

Please add comments or suggestions for sales support improvement:

_____

_____

_____

4. **Product Complaints/Returns Handling:**

4a) Fair Resolutions	1 2 3 4 5 6 7	1 2 3 4 5 6 7 NA
4b) Timely Resolutions	1 2 3 4 5 6 7	1 2 3 4 5 6 7 NA

Please add comments or suggestions for complaints/returns handling improvement:

_____

_____

_____

_____

_____

5. **Pricing:**

	ABC Company	Best Alternate Supplier
5a) Offer Fair and Competitive Price	1 2 3 4 5 6 7	1 2 3 4 5 6 7 NA
5b) Handling of Price Deviations	1 2 3 4 5 6 7	1 2 3 4 5 6 7 NA
5c) Communication of Price Changes	1 2 3 4 5 6 7	1 2 3 4 5 6 7 NA
5d) Pricing Process Meets Your Needs	1 2 3 4 5 6 7	1 2 3 4 5 6 7 NA

Please add comments or suggestions for sales support improvement:

_____

_____

_____

_____

6. **Perceived Value:**   1 2 3 4 5 6 7   1 2 3 4 5 6 7 NA

When you consider the prices that are charged for products and services, how do you rate ABC Company and your best alternate supplier in terms of value?

7. **Overall Satisfaction:**   1 2 3 4 5 6 7   1 2 3 4 5 6 7 NA

Considering all aspects of product, service, and value, how do you rate ABC Company and your best alternate supplier in terms of overall satisfaction?

8. **Best Alternate Supplier:**

Who is your best alternate supplier of widgets?

9. **Additional Comments:**

_____

_____

_____

_____

10. **Respondent Identification:**

Name: _____   Company: _____

Now, note that the first two pages of the questionnaire (the two pages the customer will see when he opens up the survey booklet) feature a list of attributes (such as Delivery) vertically on the left hand side. The specific attributes that we measure vary from survey to survey, depending on which ones our client thinks is important to look at.

The next vertical column over asks for a rating on the performance by our client on each one of those attributes; and the last column over then asks for that attribute rating for whomever the customer considers to be the Best Alternate Supplier (BAS) (and, by the way, in our next chapter, I will explain in more detail the reasoning behind PMG's seven-point scale when I share the normative results we have calculated from the thousands of survey answers we have received over the past 2 decades).

We lay out the questionnaire this way because we want the customer to rate our client in each attribute, and immediately thereafter, the BAS for the same attribute. If the customer does all the attribute rankings for our client at once, and *then* all the attribute rankings for the BAS, they will not necessarily link our client's performance as closely with the BAS's performance—so the scores will not be as accurate. It is this head-to-head rating that is critical to understanding true competitive position.

For example, they may score our client as a "6" for Delivery and the BAS a "5." That is the critical information we want, even though it may seem like our client only has a small edge over their top competitor. That small edge is enough. It is like the old story of the bear chasing two guys; the survivor does not have to run that fast, he just has to run faster than the guy next to him!

You should also note that the questionnaire groups the attributes in categories. In the sample we have reproduced in this chapter, for example, you will see categories of Product Performance Quality, Delivery & Customer Service, Sales Support, Products Complaint/Returns Handling and Pricing—with anywhere from two to five attributes grouped underneath each category heading.

We do this because we are dealing with a B2B audience. If we just put down the list of 20 or 30 attributes in a row, with no rhyme or reason, the questionnaire does not look thought out or logical. Business executives are not going to put up with that nonsense.

Breaking the attributes down into categories accomplishes two different objectives. First of all, it helps the person taking the survey to switch gears between the categories and get into the mind-set of each grouping, so they can carefully consider different aspects of the relationship. Secondly, it also demonstrates that we have "covered the waterfront" in surveying all facets of the customer-supplier connection—so the customers can see that we really want to make sure we fully understand how they feel about each one of those areas.

On the back page of the questionnaire, we frequently ask a few open-ended questions that our client is interested in having answered, in such areas as new product development, strategic direction, and particular performance issues that are important.

These questions, like the specific attributes, vary from survey to survey; for example, one client was worried about the low usage of his company's website—they were not getting the traffic they wanted. So we asked a couple questions about the website: Was it helpful? Where did it fall short? How did it compare with other websites that the customer liked and used frequently? The feedback helped the client refine the website and make it more useful to his customers.

You may also notice on the questionnaire that one of the very last questions we ask is *who* they consider to be our client's Best Alternate Supplier. We do not ask them that question upfront, even though we start asking them to rate the performance of that Best Alternate Supplier.

The reason is because the identity of the BAS can be perceived as sensitive information; if we ask right away, that could put off the survey taker. This way, we lead the customer through the whole rating exercise—and *then* ask, in an "Oh, by the way...." manner, who they think of as the supplier's BAS. In most cases, people are comfortable by this point in the questionnaire and are willing to reveal the BAS name. And, to be honest, in the B2B world, most suppliers already *know* who a customer considers to be their BAS. Since their sales people visit the customers a few times a year at the very least, they are aware who else the customers buy from.

ANSWERING THE THREE CRITICAL QUESTIONS

The objective of our customer insight surveys, as we discussed in Chapter 4, is to answer these three critical questions for our clients:

- Performance: How well are they performing compared to customer expectations?
- Importance: What attributes are most important to their customers?
- Competition: What is their competitive position in the marketplace?

It should come as no surprise then that we designed the questionnaire around those three key questions, beginning with performance. That question gets answered very directly by customers when we ask them to rank our client on how well they perform in the individual attributes with our seven-point scale, using the anchor points "1," meaning Complete Dissatisfaction, and "7," meaning Complete Satisfaction.

It is also important to note that customers are scoring these attributes based on their *expectations*, not necessarily on what the supplier's *actual performance* is. To explain further, let us use Delivery as an example. The supplier might take 2 minutes or 2 years to deliver an order—it does not matter. If the orders get there when the customer expects them to, that customer is satisfied with the supplier's performance. If the orders come at a time that the customer perceives as being late, the customer will not be happy about this particular attribute. What matters is how our client is performing compared to what the customer expects, not how the supplier actually performs—so the scoring is very subjective.

When it comes to importance, our second critical question, there are actually two different ways to measure that component. The first method is simple; we could just directly ask on the survey how important each attribute is to the customer on yet another seven-point scale. This may seem the most direct way to get this data, but it also has a couple of big problems attached to it. Number one, it involves a whole extra set of rankings that the customers have to complete—and we want to keep the work involved in filling out the questionnaire to a minimum.

The other problem with asking someone directly to rate the relative importance of something is that it is hard for them to answer accurately. It is not a matter of being dishonest or evasive, it is just a psychological roadblock. People often do not realize how important—or, conversely, unimportant—an attribute might be. They do not necessarily (or consciously) understand the real value of an attribute, something we have discussed previously in this book.

In most cases they will respond that every attribute is important—thinking that if they rate any attribute low in importance, it will be taken away from them. This results in very little distinction between attributes; when everything is important, how do you distinguish what is truly important?

That is why we use a different method of measuring importance—derivation. On every questionnaire, we always ask for an overall rating, on our seven-point scale, of the customer's "Overall Satisfaction" with the supplier. That Overall Satisfaction ranking then becomes a dependant variable that we can use to compute the correlation of the attribute's importance. Correlation is a simple and widely used measure of the relationship between two variables—in this case, each attribute and overall satisfaction. It is expressed on a zero to one scale where a zero indicates no correlation and a one indicates perfect correlation.

Attributes with a high correlation move in concert with overall satisfaction. When they are scored higher, overall satisfaction is scored higher, and vice versa. Attributes with a low correlation move independently of overall satisfaction. For example, they could be rated high and satisfaction rated low. Correlation identifies those attributes that are likely drivers of satisfaction since they are moving in parallel. I often liken it to the depression of an accelerator pedal and the speed of a car. They both move together and, all things being equal, the more you press the accelerator, the faster the car goes.

On each survey, as already noted, the list of attributes will vary, the categories of those attributes will vary and the open-ended questions will vary—but Overall Satisfaction is *always* there as a tool for us to derive importance.

Let us move on to critical question number three—competitive position. We derive that net score from the attribute rankings the customers give our client's BAS and comparing it to the rankings given to our client. The gap between those rankings provides the net score which demonstrates to the supplier where exactly it stands against the competition.

RESPONSE RATE AND THE IMPORTANCE OF FOLLOW-UP

A crucial issue that comes up with a B2B customer survey, as opposed to a consumer survey, is that you must have a high response rate or your results will suffer. That is because, again, we are dealing with small customer populations in the B2B world—and, in order to have a statistically reliable sample for a small population, you have to have a very high response rate.

The easiest way to think about this is to take it to an extreme; let us say a client only has five customers—and only three of them complete the survey. Now, someone might think that was fantastic, because you got a 60% response rate. But no, that is 40% of your customer base that you have not heard from. And, if you have that few customers, each of them suddenly becomes a lot more important when it comes to needing their feedback. If those two customers that did not respond have perceptions of performance that differ from the three that did respond, the results of the survey would be dramatically different by including them.

When you take this situation to the other extreme—say, you have got a few million people you want to do customer research on—you only need to sample around 220 of them to get a 95% confidence level in your results. In other words, you can have a response rate that is so small, it is equivalent to zero—but still have the same statistical significance. This is more the case with a consumer survey, where you could easily be dealing with a million-plus customer base.

Figure 5.1 illustrates this concept by showing the number in your survey population versus the number of responses needed to generate an equivalent level of statistical reliability.

Typically, with our B2B customer insight surveys, we are dealing with sample sizes that are anywhere from 50 to a few hundred people. When that is the case, we generally need to have response rates that are 50% or higher to get a representative sample; however, the rate we always shoot for is over 70% because each customer is so important to a supplier. That response rate is usually attainable, although, over the past 2 decades, we have seen a small but steady decline in the number of responses to our surveys. The biggest reason we hear for this decline? People just do not have the time anymore to deal with a survey!

Even though we do manage an over 70% response rate, we can still find ourselves missing important input. That is because, in the B2B arena, it is not just about statistical significance—it is also about *customer* significance. We have had surveys with a 75% response rate that were questioned by the client, simply because we could not get one critical customer contact to respond. This is an issue you will never hear about in the consumer world. No company ever goes back to the research firm and asks, "Hey, how come we never heard from Cindy Jenkins in Poughkeepsie about what she thought of our new diet soft drink?"

Fortunately, we *do* get the required response rate—and then some—to provide reliable data. But we also make it a point to do the necessary follow-up to our initial mailings to make sure we are doing everything we can to get every customer to respond.

If we have not received a survey back in a certain amount of time, then we call the customer directly to see if we can do the survey over the phone. But, again, we do not cold call—because we never assume that, when we call, an executive will have a half hour or so to spend on the phone answering questions about our client. Instead, we call to set up an appointment to talk through the survey over the phone.

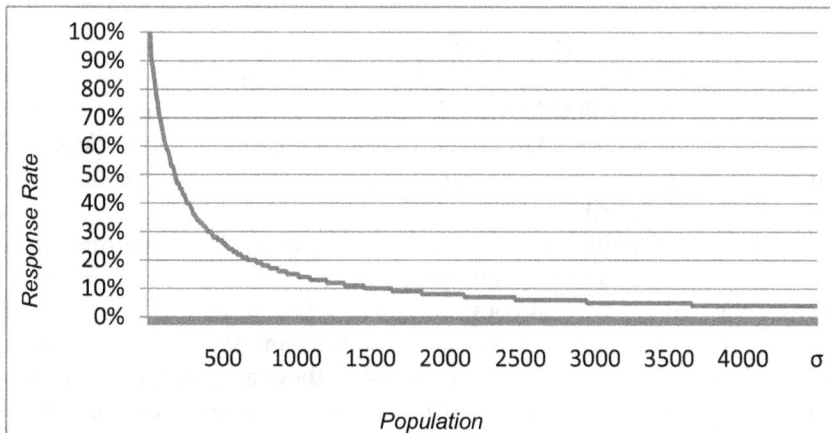

Figure 5.1.   Response rate by size survey population.

Sometimes that appointment does not happen. When we talk to the executives in question, they might say something like, "Well, I am going to be on a flight to Europe in a couple of days, I will take the questionnaire with me on the plane and do it then." Or they might want to have other managers inside the company do the specific sections that relate to their departments, then have the last guy mail the survey back to us.

Still others like to do the survey by email—so we will send them an email reminder with an embedded PDF of the survey. They just click on the PDF link, fill it out and send it back to us. We frankly do not care how we get the survey information—by phone, fax, mail or carrier pigeon, whatever works—but we do understand the importance of having a variety of response mechanisms available, because every one of these executives has different preferences for doing this kind of thing. It is our job to give them this multiplicity of options, so they can pick the one with which they are most comfortable and is easiest for them. That is absolutely key to getting the highest possible response rate.

I have to say, though, that telephone still seems to be the communication vehicle of choice. They may not actually do the survey verbally when we call, but many times, it feels like they may never do it at all, if we do not call and remind them to!

There are also times when the survey is complete, but valuable comments and explanations are left out. In those instances, we will call and say, "Hey, we noticed you rated ABC Company low on Delivery, would you mind discussing the reasons behind that?" They will hopefully explain, we will write down their answers—and also take advantage of that opportunity to ask a few more in-depth questions, such as "Is there any other area where the company can improve? And where are they doing well? Tell me that...."

That kind of unstructured and informal conversation, where we are able to find out more about why they rated some attributes as they did, is actually as or more valuable than the attribute rankings themselves. That is because you learn the "Why" behind those scores and get to understand what is really going on. These kinds of talks really become the "meat on the bones" of the attribute scores.

Of course, sometimes it does not go that smoothly. Sometimes it is extremely difficult to get in touch with the person responsible for completing the survey. We will continue to call—but we have a strict rule of leaving only two messages. Those could be voice messages on their phone or actual messages left with an assistant—but they can only add up to two. The reason is that we have found that there is a perception that, if we leave more messages than two, we risk crossing the line from professional peers to annoying callers.

Again, we want to avoid any negative connotations that would reflect badly on our client, so we will continue to call—we might call back 25 times or so—but we will leave only those couple of messages.

This kind of unavailability is something that happens with key individuals—they might be out on maternity leave, they may be in Asia somewhere overseeing a new facility and can not respond, or they might be involved in a large strategic project for a few weeks. You keep trying, but, for whatever reason, they are ultimately unable to do the survey in your needed timeframe. Our best chance for success in these cases, and another one of our secrets, is applying patient perseverance to our attempts at contact. We let them know that, when they are ready to respond, we are there and available by whatever method and at whatever time of day.

What it comes down to is this: you can not force people into completing a survey, even though a lot of companies try to do just that. In many cases, they just pick up the phone and call with no advance warning—not even an announcement letter informing the customer of what is going on. If the company does happen to get the executive on the phone, they immediately launch into the survey as if they are a telemarketer and just caught you at home. Frankly, it is an arrogant approach and one we would never inflict on our clients' customers.

I have had countless conversations with those customers myself, and, at some point during the call, I find that the customer will begin talking to me as if I am actually the supplier instead of the researcher. The customer will say, "Well, you could improve this" or "You do that very well," forgetting that I am not really going to do anything—I am not with that company! We do, however, respect the fact that that transition happens and that we do, in fact, become our client in the customers' eyes. We realize that whatever we say or however we act is a direct reflection back on our client—so we always want to be careful.

This is basically the process and customer insight survey design that we have used throughout the entire existence of PMG. It absolutely works and we only make minor adjustments when they are obviously needed.

The reason it has worked so well is that we made sure to do our homework in advance, before we sent out even one survey. What differentiates us from other marketing consultants is that the principals in our firm came from the business world. As a matter of fact, we were purchasers of consulting before we actually became consultants. And we already had the research expertise in place—we just need to make sure our approach was right in the eyes of our clients' customers. By taking the time to create the proper foundation for our customer insight survey in advance, we managed to build a durable and effective template for our clients.

In our next chapter, I am going to begin sharing PMG's results from implementing these surveys over the past 20 years. You will see that those results will reveal some very surprising and timeless truths about doing business in the B2B world.

CHAPTER 6

PMG CUSTOMER INSIGHT NORMATIVE RESULTS

> I would not say PMG's customer insight is idiot-proof … but it is pretty close.
>
> —Mike Reed
> Director of Marketing
> Bob Barker Company

BOB BARKER CASE STUDY: ONGOING INSIGHT BREEDS ONGOING SUCCESS

Bob Barker is a superstar.

Now, I am not talking about the former host of "The Price is Right," I am talking about the CEO of Bob Barker Company, a business that provides supplies to correctional facilities. You may not know this Bob Barker, but plenty of people in this particular industry do. At trade shows, attendees are familiar with being given "I ♥ Bob Barker" tote bags by the company—and then lining up to get Bob's autograph on those bags as well.

That is due to Bob's innate charisma and showmanship—he knows how to make an impact. And he also knows how to run a powerhouse company. Their performance rankings by their customers consistently put them in the top 10% of all the clients in our database. They also have earned an incredible 40% share of their specific market.

B2B Customer Insight: The Proven Path to Growth, pp. 77–91
Copyright © 2012 by Information Age Publishing
All rights of reproduction in any form reserved.

On a head-to-head basis, BBC exceeds competitive levels of performance on all attributes:

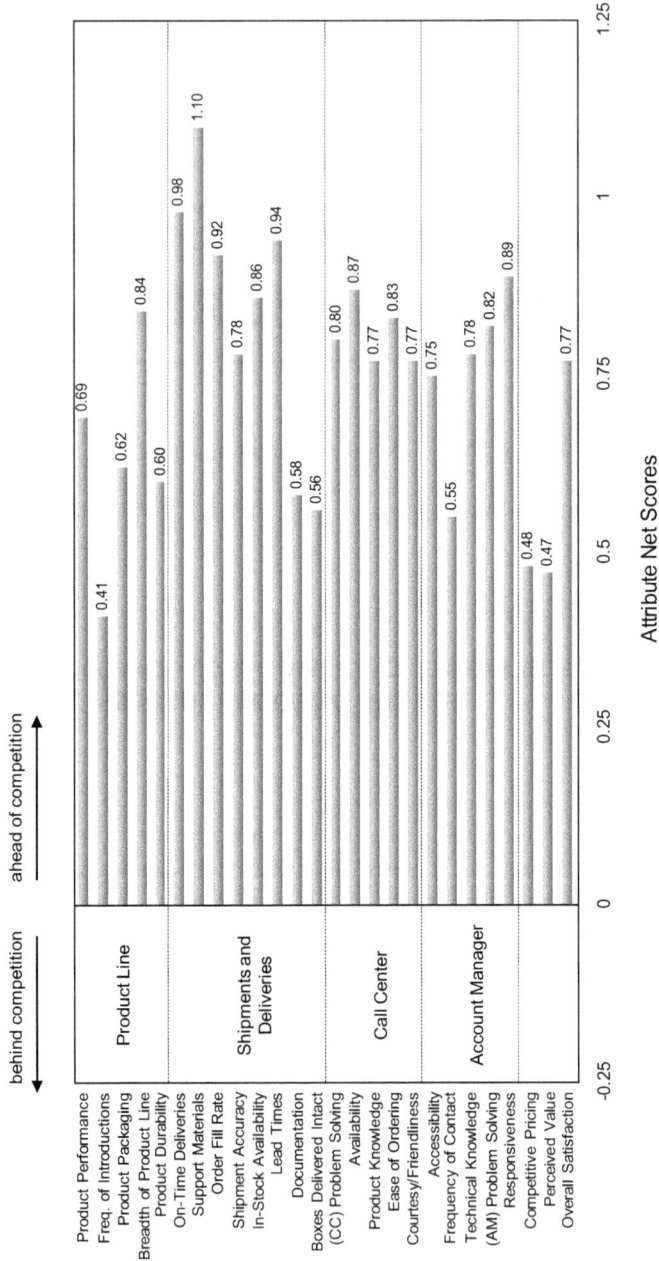

Figure 6.1. 2004 PMG study, shows BBC's compelling competitive edge.

Now, many companies sitting this pretty would think that they knew as much as they possibly could about their customers and their industry. Therefore, they might stop worrying about staying competitive or making sure their customers were receiving the value they required. Being number one means you can relax a little, right?

Well, The Bob Barker Company knows better than to sit on its laurels. From the very beginning, they have put a firm emphasis on customer insight—and all of us at PMG have been fortunate to be entrusted with delivering that crucial data to them since 1999. I will let Mike Reed, the BBC's Director of Marketing explain just how his company uses customer insight on an ongoing basis to both stay competitively sharp and to continually expand its already impressive market share.

> When I came to BBC, I was very familiar with this type of research. A monthly PMG study was already in place. These reports allowed us to track month-to-month our performance versus our key competition.
>
> Those reports continue to this day. We pride ourselves on being a metrics-driven company—and we are all provided with a companywide scorecard, from the ongoing PMG reports, that we track. Every now and then, we will see a score go down, we will frantically call John, and he will calm us down, telling us we should not worry until we see that trend continue over 2 or 3 months.
>
> In my positions with other companies prior to BBC, I worked with a lot of different research companies. There are two things I particularly like about John's team. Number one is their can-do attitude and demeanor—we will frequently call them up with immediate requests and they are willing to accommodate them. Number two is their statistical soundness. John is very knowledgeable in that area and very reliable. PMG can tell you what the data says and does not say. They also have a thorough understanding of our customer base.
>
> We operate in a market where it is hard to get customer feedback on what is happening. The PMG monthly survey provides an immediate snapshot of what is going on in our marketplace and keeps us in touch with our customers and how our performance continually measures up.
>
> —Bob Barker
> Bob Barker Company

It is a pleasure to work with a company like BBC. I regard it as being a "Curvebuster"—someone who always aces the test and skews the normative averages. The strength of BBC's relationships with their customers is amazing—and is further enabled by their intelligent use of the customer insight surveys we deliver to them on a regular basis.

Just as the Bob Barker Company has learned a great deal of general truisms about its business from using our customer insight surveys over the past 2 decades, all of us at PMG have also been able to "crunch the numbers" from the thousands of surveys we have done for multiple suppliers in a wide range of industries—and to produce some normative findings that may surprise the readers of this book.

This information, centered around the three critical questions we discussed in Chapter 4, has not been shared with the general public before now. While we will not be giving everything away in this chapter, we will reveal some significant findings, based on both the quantitative and the qualitative data we generate, that we have uncovered as a result of our 2 decades of survey work. In the next chapter, we will take this process to the final step and reveal what we believe to be the important takeaways from these normative results.

This kind of customer satisfaction normative data is rarely seen and difficult to find outside the inner sanctums of individual companies. In fact, many businesses would pay big money for this kind of information. I feel, however, that sharing these findings is important in order to discuss this subject matter as fully as possible and advance the state of the art in customer insight. In any event, whatever your business happens to be, I think you will find these discoveries as fascinating as we did when we made them.

PERFORMANCE NORMS

In the previous chapter, I gave you a look at a sample of what our survey questionnaire looks like. If you will remember, in that questionnaire, we ask the customers we are surveying to rate the performance of our supplier clients across 20 to 25 attributes. Each attribute is rated on a scale of 1 to 7, 7 being the best. Now, that is a little unusual, as most research companies tend to use a five point scale or a ten point scale. Frankly, we found that five points does not give you enough room to adequately reflect performance, while ten points adds too much unnecessary detail to the ranking process.

To delve into this a little further, every scale has a midpoint that you might consider to reflect "average" as far as a grade goes. The truth is, most people grade *higher* than that midpoint for some reason—it is called a "left bias" (even though it takes us farther to the *right* on the scale), and it is just one of the truisms of the customer research community. This fact essentially splits your scale in half from the start—it means that people who rank something at the midpoint (3.5 of our 7-point scale) are actually giving you a *very low* grade, not an average one.

This results in a situation where the vast majority of respondents are giving number judgments that land between the midpoint of the scale and the high point. In our case, between 4 and 7 is where the real action happens. Now, if we only used a five point scale, people would mostly be grading between 3 and 5—that leaves only one real point, 4, left for a score that is less than perfect. With a ten point scale, you have a lot more choices between the midpoint and 10—but we have found that it unnecessarily complicates the scoring process for those taking a survey; they do not really *need* that many choices, so it confuses the issue. A seven point scale, on the other hand, has proven over time to provide the perfect range for these kinds of surveys.

Keeping all the above in mind, our database, which is composed of surveys that use a 7-point scale, which offer an opportunity to rate a best alternate supplier and are done in a strictly B2B context, shows an average of the survey averages of **5.72**. This is illustrated in the following graph.

Notice how tight this distribution is—this is what statisticians call variance. Basically, any customer insight survey average will be between 4.7 and 6.7. So, although our database average is 5.72, a survey score of 5.3 is very low and a score of 6.2 is very high. (See Figure 6.2).

Since statistical theory tells us that a histogram of averages will follow a normal curve, we can compute percentile performance placement for any survey average score. That means we know that a score of 6.23 is at the 90th percentile—90% of companies executing the same survey under the same circumstances will score below 6.23 and only 10% will score above that.

Aggregate > Average Ratings > PMG Norm

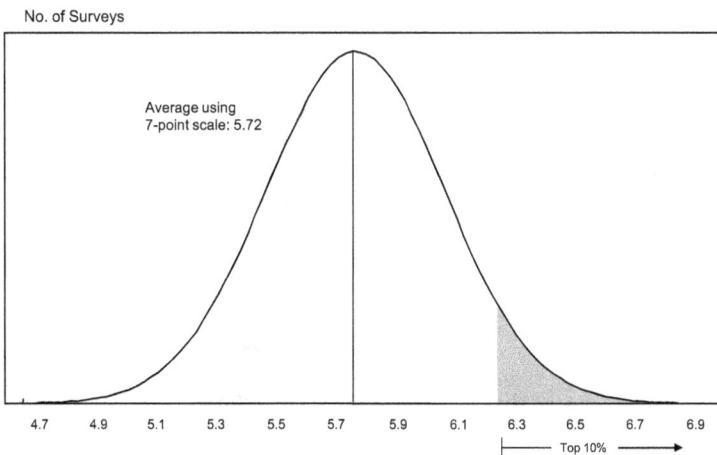

No. of Surveys

Average using
7-point scale: 5.72

4.7   4.9   5.1   5.3   5.5   5.7   5.9   6.1   6.3   6.5   6.7   6.9

Top 10%

Figure 6.2.   Distribution of survey average scores.

As you will notice, we show on the chart where the top 10% of companies perform—this is the area where companies like Bob Barker routinely place with performance scores. Now, let us go a little deeper into the individual performance attributes that PMG measures.

Over time, we have come to realize that, although each individual company will want different performance attributes to be measured, we have been able to correlate and combine many of these attributes into a common list. For example, such separate attributes as Meeting Specs, Adhering to Specs, and Consistently Achieving Specs can all be easily put under the umbrella of "Adherence to Specs."

By continuing that process, we have collapsed our clients' very large combined list of 200 to 300 attributes into 26 that are relatively common to each supplier. You will find that list below. Almost every survey we conduct also includes the attribute, "Overall Satisfaction," which is not only an overall indicator of performance, but serves as a dependent variable for determining importance—as we discussed in the last chapter.

Now, because of the extensive database PMG has on these attributes (for example, we have over 10,000 ratings of overall satisfaction, 25,000 ratings of product performance, etc.), we can state with confidence certain statistical facts about these attributes. For example, the four attributes that are most frequently used in surveys, by the request of our clients, are:

Introduction > Attributes

Adherence (to Spec.)	Documentation
Appearance	Equipment & Systems
Consistency	Marketing Support
Innovation & Design	On-Time Deliveries
Overall Product Quality	Order Lead Times
Performance	Packaging & Labeling
Product Line	Personal Service
Accessibility	Responsiveness
Accuracy	Sales Representation
Business Relationship	Technical Service
Communication	Price
Complaint Handling/Resolution	Perceived Value
Condition of Goods	Overall Satisfaction
Customer Service	

Figure 6.3.   Frequently used attributes.

1. Product performance
2. Customer service
3. Responsiveness
4. Sales representation

Figure 6.4 includes a chart featuring the aggregate average ratings of each of the 26 common attributes that are featured on our survey questionnaires (along with the above mentioned Overall Satisfaction attribute).

From this chart, you can see which attributes are usually ranked the lowest by customers—and which receive the highest ratings. Generally speaking, "Price" ends up getting the lowest marks—most customers just are not happy with the cost of the products they buy from suppliers (surprise!). Ranking second lowest is Marketing Support, while Innovation and Design ranks third lowest. Overall, this would tend to suggest that these three areas are attributes are weaknesses that most B2B suppliers suffer from, in the eyes of their customers.

Now, let us look at the *highest* rated attributes for B2B suppliers—the biggest strengths they tend to demonstrate (or, at least, are the most noticed by the customers). The single highest rated attribute is Customer Service. As we noted in Chapter 3, usually one person is responsible for this stellar rating—whoever is in charge of servicing the customer's account at the supplier's end. This is the person who the customer relies on to understand what the customer needs, knows how to handle any order problems and even knows when to give the customer a heads-up if she sees a potential problem coming down the line. Obviously having the right person in this position is critical to a supplier's customer relationship. The second highest ranked attribute by customers similarly has to do with human interactions; Personal Service.

IMPORTANCE NORMS

Now, let's move on to the normative results of our second critical component of customer insight, importance. With importance, we are able to also calculate the average score of each of our 26 common attributes to the customers we have surveyed over the years, just as we calculated the strongest and weakest performance rankings of those attributes. Importance, in contrast to performance, runs on a zero to one scale—and the overall average is .375.

Figure 6.5 breaks down those attributes in order of highest importance to lowest importance, according to those customers.

Aggregate > Average Ratings

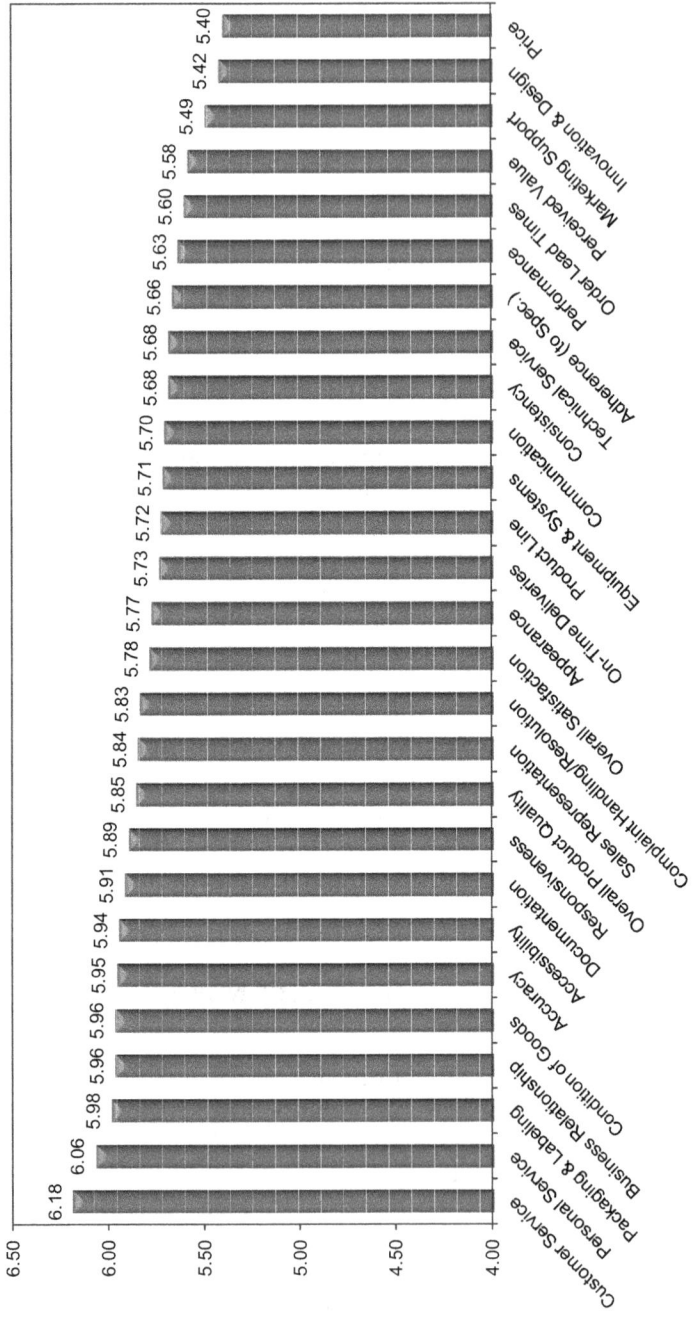

Attribute	Rating
Customer Service	6.18
Personal Service	6.06
Packaging & Labeling	5.98
Business Relationship	5.96
Condition of Goods	5.96
Accuracy	5.95
Accessibility	5.94
Documentation	5.91
Responsiveness	5.89
Overall Product Quality	5.85
Sales Representation	5.84
Complaint Handling/Resolution	5.83
Overall Satisfaction	5.78
Appearance	5.77
On-Time Deliveries	5.73
Product Line	5.72
Equipment & Systems	5.71
Communication	5.70
Consistency	5.68
Technical Service	5.68
Adherence (to Spec.)	5.66
Performance	5.63
Order Lead Times	5.60
Perceived Value	5.58
Marketing Support	5.49
Innovation & Design	5.42
Price	5.40

Figure 6.4. Average attribute ratings.

84

Aggregate > Attribute Importance

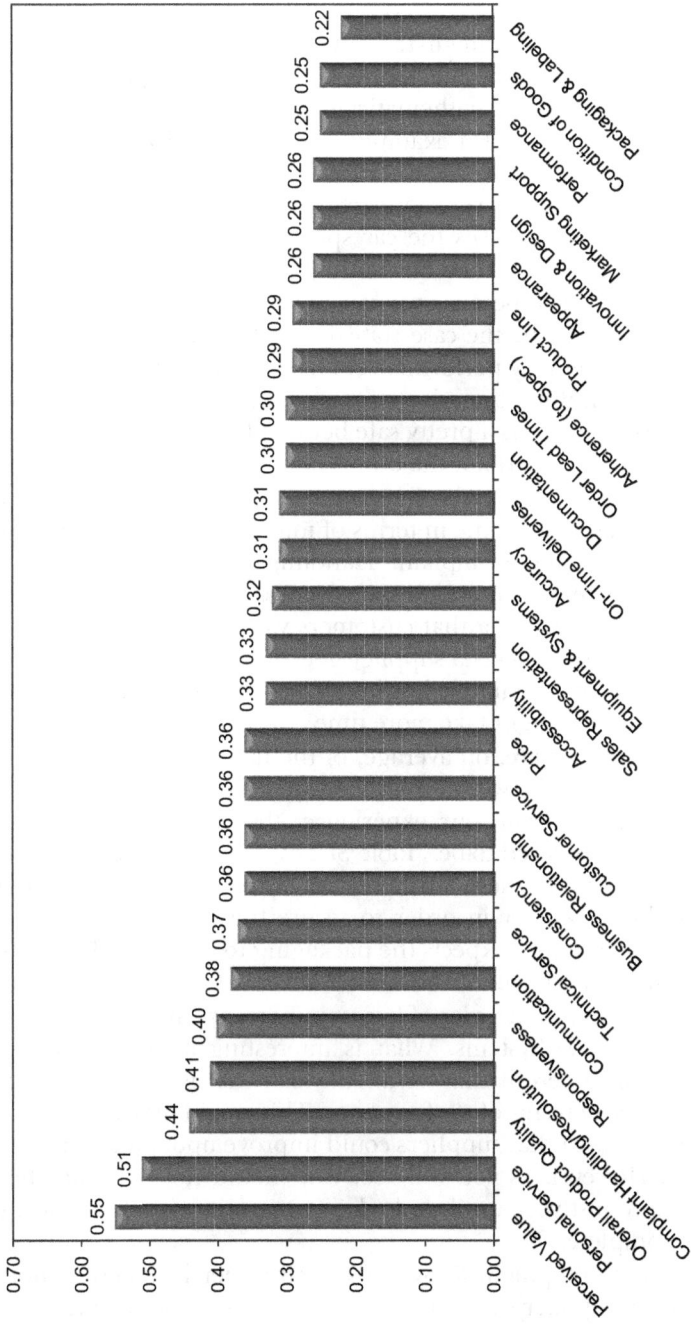

Figure 6.5. Average attribute importance.

Attribute	Value
Perceived Value	0.55
Personal Service	0.51
Overall Product Quality	0.44
Complaint Handling/Resolution	0.41
Responsiveness	0.40
Communication	0.38
Technical Service	0.37
Consistency	0.36
Business Relationship	0.36
Customer Service	0.36
Price	0.36
Accessibility	0.33
Sales Representation	0.33
Equipment & Systems	0.32
Accuracy	0.31
On-Time Deliveries	0.31
Documentation	0.30
Order Lead Times	0.30
Adherence (to Spec.)	0.29
Product Line	0.29
Appearance	0.26
Innovation & Design	0.26
Marketing Support	0.26
Performance	0.25
Condition of Goods	0.25
Packaging & Labeling	0.22

As you can see, "Perceived Value" is regarded as the most important attribute in terms of the average scores of the customers we have surveyed. Now, your immediate reaction to that might be, "Wow, if we deliver the best Perceived Value, we will deliver the highest customer satisfaction." The truth is, mathematically we can not say that—correlation does not imply causality. For example, when you are driving a car, you may turn up the radio as the car goes faster. That means the volume will be louder as the speed of the vehicle increases; that, of course, does *not* mean the volume actually makes the car speed up. The higher volume correlates with the speed, but does not cause it.

However, just because we can not measure causality, we can certainly infer it. It may be the case statistically that we do not know for sure that improved delivery performance, for example, will lead to higher levels of satisfaction. But if there is a strong correlation between delivery and overall satisfaction, it is a pretty safe bet that better delivery is a cause of overall satisfaction, and not the other way around.

Continuing down the line, we can see that Personal Service is right behind Perceived Value in terms of importance, followed by Overall Product Quality, and Complaint Handling/ Resolution. What is interesting about the next attribute, Responsiveness, is that it lags behind Complaint Handling, indicating that customers value a successful complaint resolution over how quickly a supplier gets back to them. In other words, a feeble quick fix is definitely less important than receiving a real solution to a problem that might take more time.

If the above are, on average, of the highest importance to a customer, the attributes of lowest importance are Packaging & Labeling and Product Performance. From our experience, that is because those two are frequently considered to be "Table Stakes," a concept we discussed in the last chapter; both of these attributes are *expected* to be performed at a certain level by a supplier in order to secure the customer's business. In other words, a customer expects the packaging to be acceptable and expects the product to perform, or they would not buy from you in the first place.

The next two in order of lowest importance are Marketing Support and Equipment & Systems. What is interesting about Marketing Support's appearance here is that we already saw that it ranked among the lowest attributes in terms of performance. This would indicate that, even though this is an area that suppliers could improve upon, it is still not a high priority. However, as you will see, you should not write off this particular attribute just yet—until we look at competitive performance, the story is not complete.

As for Equipment & Systems, a customer is generally not concerned with the supplier's machinery and facilities. It can be nice and appealing if the supplier has a state of the art, hi-tech factory, but as long as the customer gets a good product at a reasonable price, it is not that big a deal in terms of the business relationship. They are not paying for the supplier's factory, they are paying for their goods and/or services.

The next two low-ranked attributes are Condition of Goods and Innovation & Design. Condition of Goods is another example of "Table Stakes" (if the product does not arrive in good shape, the shipment would be rejected), while Innovation & Design, like Marketing Support, is a low-rated performance attribute that just does not really matter all that much to the customer. They do not really need a huge creative component from the supplier they use, unless that supplier constantly comes up with things that are going to help the customer sell more of their own product.

COMPETITIVE POSITION NORMS

Our third critical component of customer insight, competitive position, helps us begin to fit all the pieces of our data together.

As we noted in Chapter 4, our competitive position numbers focus on the net scores—a positive number means the supplier is getting a higher average ranking than the competition, a negative number means the customer believes the supplier is being outperformed by the competition in that particular attribute.

Before we continue, it is important to note a certain anomaly about competitive position and customer insight surveys. Forty percent of the customers in our B2B survey group do not rate a supplier against any competing company. In the large majority of the cases, that is because the supplier is regarded as the sole source of the product it sells to the customer in question; either the customer does not know of an alternative company or chooses to only buy from the supplier in question. We do not know exactly how many of that 40% that is the case with, but, judging from customer survey comments and our own knowledge of our clients' customer base, this is very often the situation.

The PMG norm net score for competitive position is 0.23, as you can see in Figure 6.6.

Again, notice the low variance in this distribution. Essentially all of the scores run from -0.6 to 1.0. Just as with the curve for survey average scores, relatively small differences can have huge implications on the position of the company in the marketplace.

Now, let us go ahead and break down our aggregate norm scores for the individual attributes in terms of competitive position. In this case, the Figure 6.7 shows that the number one attribute customers say suppliers do better than the competition is a pretty big surprise.

Aggregate > Net Score > PMG Norm

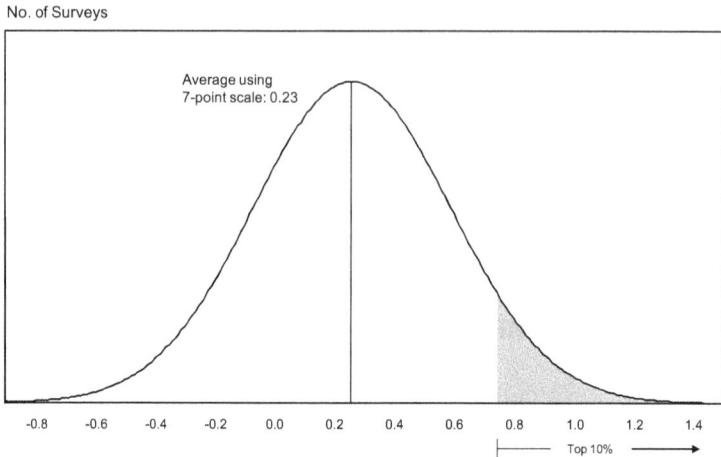

No. of Surveys

Average using
7-point scale: 0.23

| -0.8 | -0.6 | -0.4 | -0.2 | 0.0 | 0.2 | 0.4 | 0.6 | 0.8 | 1.0 | 1.2 | 1.4 |

Top 10%

Figure 6.6   Survey average net scores.

Yes, Marketing Support actually wins the competitive position trophy. If you will recall, in terms of performance, customers ranked this as one of the *worst* performing attributes of suppliers. In terms of importance, they ranked this as one of the attributes having the *least* significance. So how to explain this coming in first in terms of competitive position? Well, what the customers seem to be saying is, "We do not care about Marketing Support, you are doing a lousy job with it, but you are way better than the competition at it!"

We believe that this seemingly contradictory data stems from the fact that if a B2B supplier does *any* kind of marketing support for a product (such as attending trade shows, conducting joint sales calls with distributors, placing ads in industry magazines), the customer is mightily impressed—even if the effort is, all in all, not actually all that terrific. The main reason for being impressed, to tell the truth, is that the competition is not doing anything at all.

The Marketing Support example is a prime reason why all *three* of the critical questions—performance, importance and competitive position—need to be answered to achieve true customer insight. If we only relied on the first two, we would have completely dismissed Marketing Support as fairly meaningless. Adding the competitive position data into the mix, however, shows that you can impress a customer and complement your

Aggregate > Net Scores

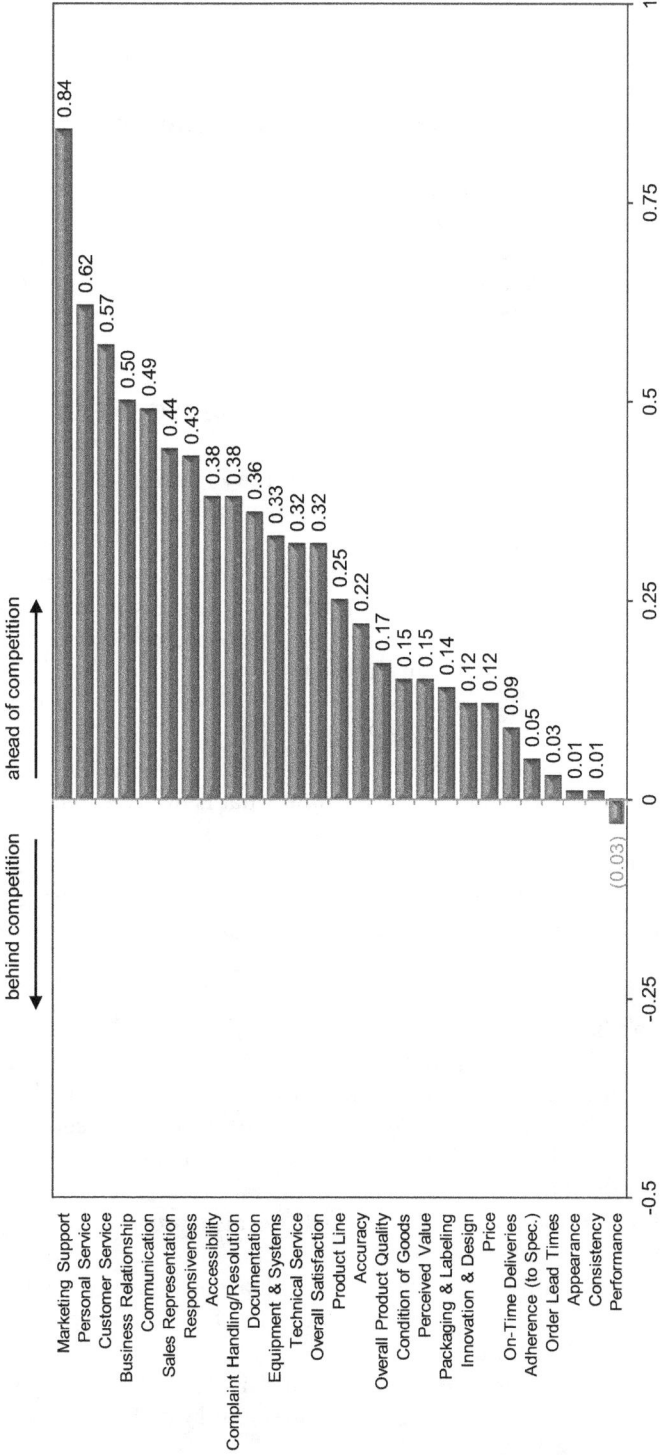

Figure 6.7.   Average net scores.

89

value and satisfaction position by investing minimal effort in marketing support.

This is a prime example of why we vigorously pursue answers to all three of our critical questions. Think of a three-legged stool that collapses if you remove one of its legs; a customer insight survey, likewise, will not stand up to scrutiny if it fails to take into account performance, importance or competitive position. With only one or two of those components in place, you risk the result of a simplistic—or just plain wrong—interpretation of the data.

BOB BARKER CASE STUDY #2: USING THE DASHBOARD

We began this chapter by looking at how The Bob Barker Company used our customer insight data on a regular basis to ensure its top-level status with its customers. As indicated, we still generate updated reports on a bimonthly basis at their request, so they can make sure nothing is falling through the cracks. As a result, they are constantly looking at their own normative results—and making sure they are not dipping from the high standards they have set in the past.

We make that process as easy as possible for them. At PMG, we believe in delivering customer insight data that is as user-friendly as possible; we do not just throw a dense complex 100 page report at someone and expect them to instantly understand what is in there. That is why the centerpiece of our bimonthly reports to them is a document that we call "The Dashboard," a visually-oriented one page information sheet that shows how BBC is performing on five important attributes over time.

Figure 6.8, which I thank The Bob Barker Company for allowing us to share with the readers of this book, is from December of 2009.

The bimonthly Dashboard is routinely shared with all the departments at Bob Barker, so they can see in a snapshot what they need to be improving on. In a flash, they can see how their performance is being currently rated in comparison to the named Best Alternate Supplier and they can also see how their net competitive position is with regard to these attributes over time. And no one has to be a statistical genius to understand the information being conveyed.

In addition to this Dashboard, we also provide Bob Barker with an individual breakout of the five attribute scores, as well as a call log complete with comments from the individual customer contacts surveyed. The questions asked vary from month to month depending on specific areas of interest to the company.

Bob Barker is one company that is accustomed to using customer insight on a regular basis. They understand which attributes are a priority

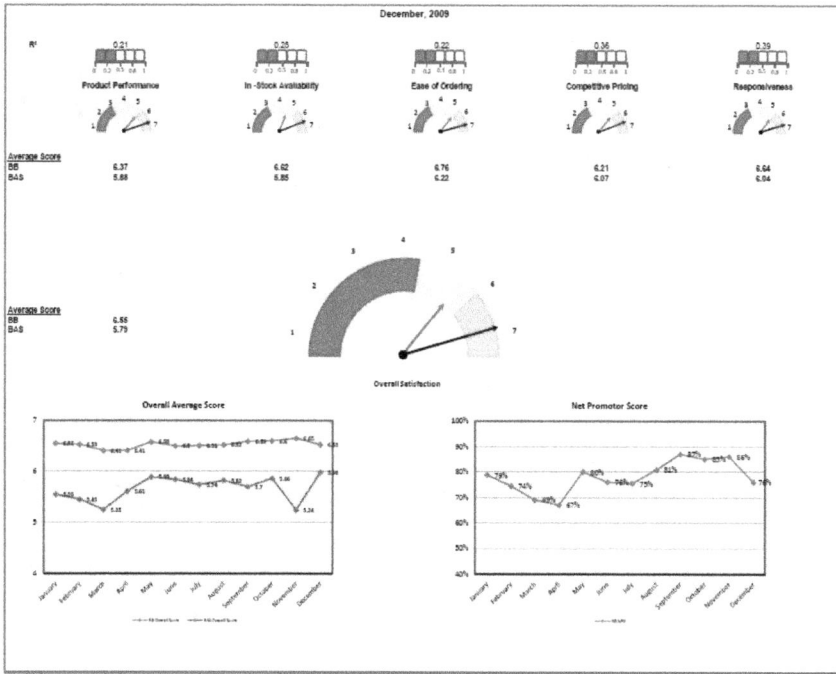

Figure 6.8. Dashboard of survey results.

to focus on in order to keep their existing market share as well as to build on it. Again, that is information that is vital to any business, but particularly in the B2B world, where there are fewer customers who individually contribute a lot more to a supplier's bottom line.

While every supplier will have unique variances in their customer insight data, depending on their particular industry and customers, PMG's normative results over the years have yielded some vital overall directions any B2B business should consider in order to experience long-term growth and success. In the next chapter, we will discuss what all our data signifies—and how those revelations are incredibly significant to suppliers around the world.

CHAPTER 7

SUCCESS THROUGH CUSTOMER INSIGHT: THE CUSTOMER-DRIVEN COMPANY

We improved our share ... and took the business away from a big, big company.

—Tim Bergwall
Vice President and General Manager
Containerboard Mills; Greif, Inc.

GREIF CASE STUDY: GOING THE WHOLE NINE YARDS WITH CUSTOMER INSIGHT, PART 1

Throughout this book, we have shared a number of case studies that demonstrated just how our clients effectively utilized the customer insight data that PMG provided to them. With the exception of our sleepy (and anonymous) CEO from the first chapter, they all implemented our results in smart and efficient ways that enabled their companies to improve their overall dealings with customers.

Our final case study, however, is truly a textbook example of how to specifically apply customer insight data to gain the maximum results. Greif Inc., a world leader in industrial packaging products and services, is a great believer in what they call "account planning;" this is a process that

B2B Customer Insight: The Proven Path to Growth, pp. 93–103
Copyright © 2012 by Information Age Publishing
All rights of reproduction in any form reserved.

involves formulating and following through on a specific sales strategy for each individual customer.

Through account planning, Greif aggressively creates opportunities for itself rather than waiting for them to appear. And, it turned out, our approach to customer insight dovetailed incredibly well with their approach to customer sales—which, subsequently, created a powerful synergy as a result. I will let Tim Bergwall, Greif's Vice President and General Manager, Containerboard Mills, relate why Greif decided we were the research company for them.

> We are huge advocates of conducting account planning processes within our company. What that means is holding a fact-based discussion with our sales representative, our sales manager and any other necessary company personnel—how we are going to approach an individual customer, what we need to do to the relationship more profitable for us, and, crucially, what we need to do to make them more profitable. We have been doing this kind of account planning for years.
>
> To further strengthen this process, we decided to do a customer needs analysis that we called 'The Voice of the Customer.' In order to accomplish this, we looked at several research companies, one of which we had actually worked with before and who assumed they were a lock to do this project.
>
> John, however, came in with samples of the PMG output they obtained for other clients. We were really impressed with their way of analyzing the customer responses in what they termed the Performance Improvement Map—we all fell in love with the idea. Having one page that merges two pieces of critical data—how important the various performance attributes are to the customer, combined with how well we are doing with those attributes relative to the next best alternative supplier—really sold us on the PMG methodology.
>
> From there, it was pretty easy. We thought it was great that these guys spent a solid half day with us just learning about our business—not talking about the survey work, just asking what our business challenges were, what drove our industry, and how did we traditionally win in our market. That made us confident that they really understood what we were all about. Moving forward, we came up with questions we wanted to ask and they helped us to design the survey instrument. Our customers gave PMG really good marks on the quality of the survey interviews, because they were conducted by knowledgeable PMG principals.
>
> PMG's big advantage was how they delivered the analytics once the survey was completed. We did not really have time to figure out the best way to interpret the data, no one at a company like ours really does. We thought PMG's follow-up was much better. They provided an expert interpretation of the data that was easy to access and understand, in large part because they had a much better insight into our business due to their own fact-finding and extensive B2B experience.

There was only one thing missing in the results PMG provided us with. Since we commissioned the survey as an overall look at all our customer relationships, we did not have data that was granular enough for our account planning. So we went back to PMG and said, 'Can we do this same Performance Improvement Map for each customer based on their individual responses?' They said, yes, they could cut the data any way we wanted. So we ended up with specific customer improvement maps.

Those maps were introduced into our account planning process—which enabled us to have some real robust discussions around what matters most to each particular customer and how we were—or were not—meeting those needs. Each discussion essentially set up for us the perfect sales call. We could now go out and meet with the customer, with their specific map in front of us, and say, "We have got 50% of your business ... what would it take to get it all? We can see we are doing a pretty good job in these areas, but not in this particular one. If we improved our performance there ... will that improve our position with you?"

With several customers, the answer was "Yes, it will." This proved to be a great and nonthreatening way to follow up with a customer and say, number one, we are listening to you, and number two, this is what we heard, is that right? And they can either validate their comments or explain what they really meant if we misunderstood.

The important thing is to get that agreement from them upfront—that if you find a way to improve a certain aspect of your performance, they will give you more business. But the other critical side of this comes from your end, and that is something we recognized early on; if you really are going to improve, it will take more than just having your sales team on board. If you want to fundamentally change your value proposition, you also need to have the appropriate operations on board as well.

So, to prepare for these customer meetings, what we did was take these specific Performance Improvement Maps into a 2-day conference. We told everyone, "Clear your plate, look in the mirror, we are going to talk overall how we are doing as a company, but then we are going to dig into specific accounts to see how we can grow them." And we make sure we have everyone in the room, the guy in charge of shipping, the scheduling and planning manager, and, critically, the mill manager. The mill manager, if you know anything about the paper industry, is typically a very powerful individual within the organization. He basically is running a small city, overseeing four hundred employees in what is perhaps a billion dollar facility. He also frequently has an engineering background and you can't win him over with anecdotal information—he wants to see data.

Anyway, we make the account plans and get everyone who will have to carry through on the improvements to agree on the plans. We left by stacking hands and saying, "Let us go get it!"

—Tim Bergwall
Vice President and General Manager
Containerboard Mills; Greif, Inc.

It is very satisfying from our perspective to work with a client who is willing to go the distance with our data. Later in this chapter, Tim will share exactly what happened from there with two of his *own* case studies— so you will be able to see just how Greif substantially grew their business by the process described above.

In addition to the nuts and bolts of their account planning process, the Greif case study also illustrates compellingly the "big picture" takeaway we have discovered from the customer insight data we have compiled over the years—a takeaway I am about to share for the first time here.

SUPPLIERS AND CUSTOMERS: WHAT MAKES THE DIFFERENCE

In the last chapter, we looked at the normative results derived from those decades of surveys. Now, we are going to take the last vital step that we always feel is necessary to any study—the all-important interpretation of that data. In this case, interpreting our overall customer insight numbers will reveal what we have discovered to be *the most important element to building successful B2B customer relationships.*

Before we do that, it is important to first understand that, from the customer's perspective, most suppliers are really, for all intents and purposes, selling the same exact products. Those products could be chemicals, packaging, equipment, distribution services or any other B2B product. Because these products are viewed as being basically equivalent, however, the customers really choose the suppliers who, they feel, know their business, understand their needs and advocate for them. If there is a problem, they are going to resolve it quickly and make good on it. By being proactive and showing concern for the customer *on a human level*, the supplier's employees create value for the customer.

You will note that one aspect of PMG's approach that really impressed Greif was that we took the time to understand *their* business before we even began the process of creating their specific survey. And that one of the complaints about the research company that preceded us was that they really did not understand what Greif's industry was all about. Not to blow our own horn, but the importance of this understanding and responsiveness to customers can not be underestimated, as we are about to see.

Below, you will find a chart we discussed briefly in our last chapter, PMG's aggregate norm scores for individual attributes in terms of competitive position. Figure 7.1 reflects 2 decades of B2B survey data. As we already discussed, the top attribute in terms of competitive position is Marketing Support. Now, I would like you to take a look at the next few attributes that are closest to that top attribute; Personal Service, Customer Service, Business Relationships (this attribute relates to a supplier's com-

Aggregate > Net Scores

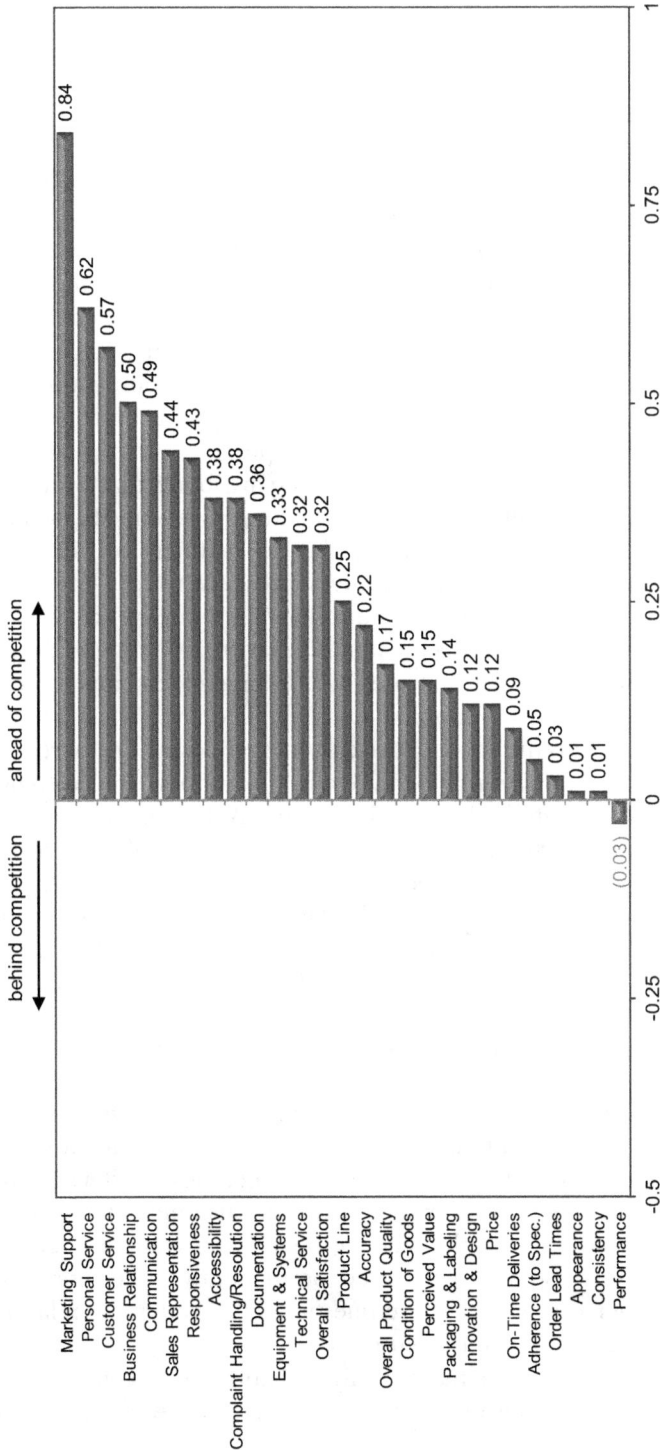

Figure 7.1. Average net scores.

mitment to the customer's particular industry, by the way), and Communication.

As a block, these were the attributes (with the noted exception of Marketing Support) where the suppliers outstripped their toughest competition the most in their customers' eyes. And, as a block, they all reflect what we already revealed in the normative data derived from our other two critical questions of Performance and Importance in the last chapter—and that is the significance of the *personal aspect* of business and how well the customer feels supported by the supplier's people.

Now, let us examine what attributes these same customers ranked *lowest* in terms of what suppliers did better than the competition. Price, Packaging & Labeling, Delivery, and a variety of product quality attributes (Consistency, Appearance, Adherence to Specs).

In other words, we are back to the attributes that comprise the "Table Stakes" quadrant of a Performance Improvement Map—those attributes that a customer expects a supplier to routinely deliver just to be taken seriously. Again, in the customers' eyes, each supplier is basically selling the same product—and if a supplier can not deliver a certain basic aspect of that product, what is the point of buying from one of them?

Now, let us take that idea to the bigger and much more important question—if every supplier *can* indeed deliver these low-ranking attributes, what is the basis for the customer choosing one particular supplier?

The real differentiator is, again, the support the customer feels from the supplier itself. And yet, how many B2B companies in their sales and marketing focus on promoting their superior quality, their investments in cutting edge factory systems, fast delivery and so forth? All those qualities may be true and may be worth bragging about. But, at the end of the day, the PMG database, which cuts across a wide range of industries and companies located all over the world, shouts loud and clear …

That is not how business is won.

This is a huge point to realize—and it all comes from customer insight. Business is won by delivering personal service that translates into value for the customer. Does the customer feel looked after? Do the supplier's sales reps and customer reps know the customer's business and advocate for the customer within the supplier's own company? Do problems get taken seriously and get solved permanently? The more affirmatively a customer can answer those questions, the better the relationship a supplier will enjoy with that customer.

At PMG, we have many, many verbatim survey comments from customers that verify this powerful and simple truth. And our Greif case study is an exemplary example of putting this truth to work in their very success-ful customer interactions.

USING CUSTOMER INSIGHT TO DIRECTLY GROW YOUR BUSINESS

As you may remember at the beginning of this chapter, Tim Bergwall from Greif discussed how important our Performance Improvement Map was to their efforts in being the perfect customer-driver company. In Chapter 4, we introduced and explained this particular survey tool and also shared a sample Performance Improvement Map based on one sample company's customer insight.

In Figure 7.2 you will find another Performance Improvement Map; this one, however, was created from the PMG statistical norms that we have been talking about in this and the last chapter. This map illustrates those aggregate averages for performance, importance and competitive position and locates them in the map quadrant in which these attributes most commonly fall.

This map, which again, condenses 20 years of data into one visual chart, confirms what we just talked about; that the overwhelming majority of real "Market Levers" in a B2B relationship are those based on personal

Aggregate > Performance Improvement Map

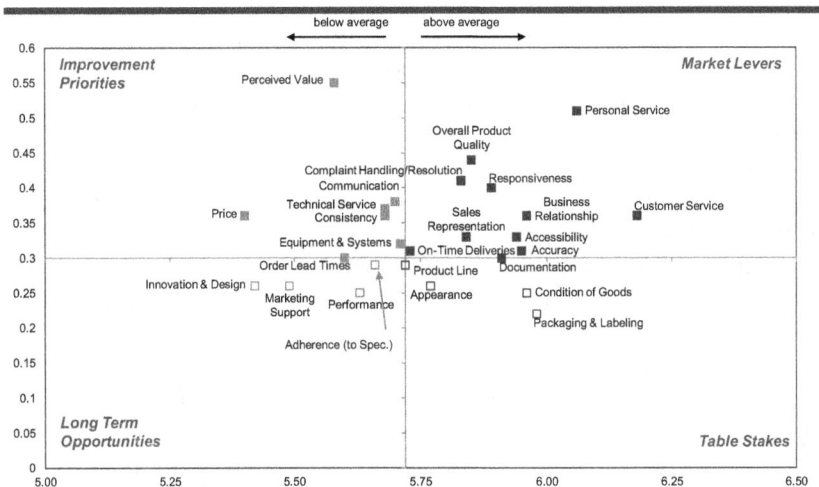

Figure 7.2.   Performance improvement map using normative data.

interactions, such as Personal Service, Customer Service, Responsive, etcetera. These are the qualities that are the most important sales points for a supplier and are recognized by the customer as the strongest areas of outstanding performance.

Again, this map is only the average of the aggregate—each customer insight survey yields its own individual Performance Improvement Map and its own unique findings. And make no mistake about it, those findings can be used to incredibly powerful ends, as Greif's case study clearly illustrates. Let us briefly discuss the specifics of why Greif's approach is so effective.

As the B2B marketplace is generally a fairly small world, customers are very aware that the supplier will know what scores the customers gave them in our surveys—as well as what specific comments they made regarding the supplier's performance. This objective, data-driven look into the customer's mind-set is, as Tim made clear, an excellent springboard for a direct and productive conversation between supplier and customer—a conversation that can be profitable for both parties.

Since the supplier knows what a specific customer is saying—and the customer knows that is the case—this creates a unique opportunity for the supplier. As Greif does, any supplier can actually go back to the customer, armed with the survey info, and say, "You said if a supplier performed better on x, y and z (whatever attributes were indicated in the specific survey), that would increase your satisfaction and value. If a supplier did that, you would give them more business. Well, we are ready to go ahead and make the investment, and significantly improve our performance in those areas. If we do that, will you commit to buying more from us?"

The customer is suddenly in a corner. He almost has to agree, because he himself set up the situation with his comments. In most cases, this initiates a very valuable and worthwhile discussion with the customer as he must either validate those comments or explain them further if he did not quite articulate his thoughts clearly enough.

You are about to read two specific examples of how Greif followed through on this exact process. I frankly do not know why more of our clients do not replicate their very focused approach. If you know *precisely why* a customer would increase their orders from you, and you can achieve a positive ROI (Return on Investment) on investments that would be necessary to make that happen, why would not you go to the customer and attempt to gain a bigger share of their business by agreeing to make the requested improvements?

The Performance Improvement Map we generate from customer insight data is just that—a map. But this is a map that shows you the precise ways to effectively build your share with existing customers. Not acting on that information is like turning away free money—and very few of us would think that was a good idea, especially these days.

GREIF CASE STUDY: GOING THE WHOLE NINE YARDS WITH CUSTOMER INSIGHT, PART 2

I am going to let Tim Bergwall relate his two case studies of how Greif made the PMG data work for them.

> PMG's Customer Insight really paid off with a couple of key customers. In a discussion of the first customer's Performance Improvement Map, the customer indicated that Greif's resources could help with their own operation—to make it more lean, increase their throughput, save energy and improve their yield on waste. We went to them and said, if we contribute this way, will you give us a better position as a supplier? They said, "Absolutely, let us come up with a way of leveraging your resources to make this happen."
>
> We flew up to their facility several times and did a complete audit of their operation and machinery. We agreed they were not equipped the way they needed to be equipped to be as efficient as possible. Greif had a machine that had a book value of about $100,000—we were not using it, it was older technology to us, but to them, it would be relatively new technology. We refurbished it and installed it at their facility at our expense. Their productivity went up and their waste went down. As a result, we picked up about $3,000,000 more in volume in very attractive markets—at a cost to us of about $150,000 to $160,000. We improved our share and took the business from a big, big company that has a lot more resources than we do.
>
> The second customer I want to talk about is a big company on the West Coast. At the time, we were selling a couple of 100 tons a month to them. We again used the Performance Improvement Map specific to this customer as the starting point to build a better relationship. In this case, there was a performance gap in the strength of our product that we were selling to them. This transitioned into a discussion of paper attributes, what they should care about what they should not care about. We found out what would make the difference to them and took it back to our own operations folks.
>
> We told our people, 'If we can give them more of this performance attribute, we can improve our position. Can we do it?' They said, 'Yeah, we can do it, but not without a cost. We will have to slow our machines down, add more chemicals, do a little more refining, those kinds of things.' We looked at the costs and calculated that the margins we got on this particular account would more than cover them—it was still a win. So we got the mill manager and all the engineers to agree to the new procedures, and went back to the customer. And we got a firm agreement that, if we did all this, we would get more business from them.

When we ran the initial order with the new specs, we published Certificates of Analysis on every roll. They all shipped overseas, where the rolls got glowing reviews, and the customer came back and awarded us about 1,300 tons a month. In other words, we picked up over a 1,000 tons a month—we are talking big, big, big dollars.

The value of this went beyond those dollars however. What we picked up was some new export business, which was really significant because of our domestic economy. Since it has not recovered yet, we knew we needed to get some export business in order to diversify and protect ourselves from dips in the domestic market. Our main competition in this arena was some European mills, whose product had a better performance than ours—they used a different fiber and more sophisticated machinery. What we did to upgrade our performance for this particular customer helped us learn that we could make modifications to our process and run a product that would be competitive with theirs.

One big positive from that is that, typically, during the holidays, we usually had to slow down. Now, we have got this new market, so we can run full-out throughout the holiday season.

Now, it is possible that in both the above cases, we might have gotten to the same answers without the customer insight survey. Might have. But the survey helps organize and bring seriousness to the discussion with the customer in two important ways. Number one—we spent money to go out and do this and that sends the right message; we care and we listened. Number two—the customer took time to answer the survey, so we both have some skin in the game. Rather than just putting this survey up on a bookshelf to collect dust, it is better to sit down and talk about it, leverage it and figure out how to do something that is to the benefit of both of us. And, to me, that is the coolest part of this whole process, that we did something more with the PMG data than say, "Hey, we got a good approval rating out of this, everything's okay."

If I was going to consult with a company and tell them how to do this, I would tell them what the two most important things are to this approach. First, you have to have alignment with your own operation to make the needed improvements. The survey helps with this factor because people tend to react better to formal studies rather than anecdotal feedback from the market. If I just walked and said, "Hey, I just got chewed out over at Acme—they are mad and we have to do shipping and quality control better," that does not fly as well as, "We just did a formalized survey and we have to improve in these areas and, by the way, if we do, we are going to grow." Sales guys sometimes get a bad rap for overreacting and being alarmist. When you wrap real concerns in an instrument like this, however, it is more scientific and taken more seriously.

Secondly, you should not waste any more time making sales calls without a defined strategy. Use the data to have a really bold conversation—"How do we improve, and if we can improve, can we grow with you?" It is a more elaborate way to ask them for an order, quite frankly, but it works.

How well does it work? Well, the question we would ask ourselves is, "Are we going to it again next year?" And the answer would be, "Damn right we are!" As a matter of fact, we have a meeting coming up, with people coming in from all over the world. We are going to share these case studies with everyone and discuss putting this kind of customer insight process in place for the entire company.

—Tim Bergwall
Vice President and General Manager
Containerboard Mills; Greif, Inc.

Thank you, Tim. And, in conclusion, I would like to point out that the secret of Greif's approach with their customers does in fact reinforce the point that the human element is the most important factor in a supplier-customer relationship.

You will note that Greif came back to the customer to discuss what they said in the survey and use it as a springboard for a more far reaching conversation. You will also notice, in both cases, Greif made sure to add value to their customer; in the first case, by actually improving the customer's physical operation for them, and, in the second case, improving the product Greif sold without any extra cost to that particular customer.

In both cases, the customers also stuck to their original agreements—and gave Greif a significant bump in business. As Tim revealed in the first case study, they took business away from a competitor that actually had significantly more resources than Greif did!

Customer insight is a tool like any other. Its value derives from how well it is used. If you, as Tim phrased it, put it on a bookshelf to collect dust, it obviously wo not do you much good. But, if you put it to work as Greif and the other companies whose stories I have told in this book did, you can not only grow your company, you can not only improve your customer relations, but, internally, you will also create energizing and unifying goals to both management and personnel.

I challenge you to get started. Begin with internal data you probably already have—sales call reports, quality records, warranty forms—whatever you have, mine that information for insight into what customers want. Then look at formalizing the customer insight process. Make sure you include the three critical questions—how are you doing, what's important and how do you stand against competition. If you can get good data in response to these three questions, you are on your way to developing deep customer insight that will in turn lead to profitable growth.

It works—I hope if nothing else, we've proven that through the examples in this book. Drop me a line and let me know how you're doing—I'd love to hear from you.

ABOUT THE AUTHOR

John Barrett received his MBA from the University of South Florida, after which he worked for the retail consulting firm, Payment Systems Inc., based in Tampa, Florida. He left the company to complete the coursework in the marketing doctoral program at the University of Virginia's Darden Graduate School of Business. He then joined Sonoco, the packaging company located in Hartsville, South Carolina, where he worked in the corporate marketing and strategic planning divisions for a total of 6 years.

In 1992, John departed from Sonoco to cofound Priority Metrics Group, Inc. (PMG) with fellow Sonoco manager Warren Hayslip. After 5 years, Warren went on to work at a variety of other firms and still employs John and PMG to perform customer insight surveys at his current company, Peerless Manufacturing, where he holds the title of COO.

John, who serves as President of PMG, has made it his mission in the 2 decades since the company's creation to perfect the implementation and application of customer insight and market assessment surveys so that his client's companies can enjoy the maximum rewards from these research tools. His areas of expertise include customer satisfaction, strategic market analysis, strategic planning, competitor analysis and mergers & acquisitions. He is also a member of ESOMAR, one of the leading international market research organizations.

John presently resides in Spartanburg, South Carolina, with his wife, Cindy McPhee-Barrett. The couple has three daughters, Sarah (24), Alix (22) and Mahria (19), who are all currently pursuing their higher education.

www.ingramcontent.com/pod-product-compliance
Lightning Source LLC
Chambersburg PA
CBHW061830220326
41599CB00027B/5250

* 9 7 8 1 6 1 7 3 5 9 8 6 6 *